Semantic Role Labeling

Synthesis Lectures on Human Language Technologies

Editor

Graeme Hirst, *University of Toronto*

Synthesis Lectures on Human Language Technologies publishes monographs on topics relating to natural language processing, computational linguistics, information retrieval, and spoken language understanding. Emphasis is placed on important new techniques, on new applications, and on topics that combine two or more HLT subfields.

Semantic Role Labeling
Martha Palmer, Daniel Gildea, and Nianwen Xue
2010

Spoken Dialogue Systems
Kristiina Jokinen and Michael McTear
2010

Introduction to Chinese Natural Language Processing
Kam-Fai Wong, Wenji Li, Ruifeng Xu, and Zheng-sheng Zhang
2009

Introduction to Linguistic Annotation and Text Analytics
Graham Wilcock
2009

Dependency Parsing
Sandra Kübler, Ryan McDonald, and Joakim Nivre
2009

Statistical Language Models for Information Retrieval
ChengXiang Zhai
2008

Semantic Role Labeling

Martha Palmer, Daniel Gildea, and Nianwen Xue

ISBN: 978-3-031-01007-1   paperback
ISBN: 978-3-031-02135-0   ebook

DOI 10.1007/978-3-031-02135-0

A Publication in the Springer series
SYNTHESIS LECTURES ON ADVANCES IN AUTOMOTIVE TECHNOLOGY

Lecture #6
Series Editor: Graeme Hirst, *University of Toronto*
Series ISSN
Synthesis Lectures on Human Language Technologies
Print 1947-4040   Electronic 1947-4059

Semantic Role Labeling

Martha Palmer
University of Colorado, Boulder

Daniel Gildea
University of Rochester

Nianwen Xue
Brandeis University

SYNTHESIS LECTURES ON HUMAN LANGUAGE TECHNOLOGIES #6

ABSTRACT

This book is aimed at providing an overview of several aspects of semantic role labeling. Chapter 1 begins with linguistic background on the definition of semantic roles and the controversies surrounding them. Chapter 2 describes how the theories have led to structured lexicons such as FrameNet, VerbNet and the PropBank Frame Files that in turn provide the basis for large scale semantic annotation of corpora. This data has facilitated the development of automatic semantic role labeling systems based on supervised machine learning techniques. Chapter 3 presents the general principles of applying both supervised and unsupervised machine learning to this task, with a description of the standard stages and feature choices, as well as giving details of several specific systems. Recent advances include the use of joint inference to take advantage of context sensitivities, and attempts to improve performance by closer integration of the syntactic parsing task with semantic role labeling. Chapter 3 also discusses the impact the granularity of the semantic roles has on system performance. Having outlined the basic approach with respect to English, Chapter 4 goes on to discuss applying the same techniques to other languages, using Chinese as the primary example. Although substantial training data is available for Chinese, this is not the case for many other languages, and techniques for projecting English role labels onto parallel corpora are also presented.

KEYWORDS

semantic roles, predicate-argument structure, Frame Elements, supervised and unsupervised semantic role labeling, machine learning, features, projection, language-independent semantic role labeling, PropBank, FrameNet, VerbNet

Contents

Preface

Analysis of semantic relations and predicate-argument structure is one of the core pieces of any system for natural language understanding. This field has a long history, but has also undergone significant change in recent years. The advent of systematically defined resources for semantic structures has enabled the creation of large corpora annotated according to these standards, and automatic systems trained using the resulting data. Given the large amount of work in this area from groups around the world, it can be difficult for the uninitiated to get a sense of the state of the art; we hope that the overview we provide in this volume will be helpful to newcomers to the field as well as to practitioners in other areas of natural language processing. While some background in computational linguistics will be helpful to the reader, we have assumed very little specific technical knowledge. We have envisioned this volume as the initial basis of a graduate seminar, possibly including a variety of students from computer science, linguistics, and related fields. We hope that it will provide an appropriate springboard for progress on the exciting new challenges we outline in our conclusion.

Much of following chapters arises from our own work in this area, and would not have been possible without our collaborators, in particular: Dan Jurafsky, Paul Kingsbury, Karin Kipper Schuler, Hoa Trang Dang, Szu-ting Yi, Edward Loper, and Julia Hockenmaier. We are also grateful to the organizers of CoNLL who have showcased this task in several consecutive meetings. Finally, we wish to thank Katrin Erk, Susan Brown and two anonymous reviewers for their comments on our draft, and Graeme Hirst for his guidance in the development and editing of the book.

Martha Palmer   Boulder, Colorado
Daniel Gildea   Rochester, New York
Nianwen Xue   Waltham, Massachusetts

December 2009

CHAPTER 1

Semantic Roles

1.1 INTRODUCTION

Robust syntactic parsers (Collins, 2000; Charniak, 2000; McDonald et al., 2005; Nivre et al., 2006) have had a major impact on the field of natural language processing in recent years. However, the syntactic analyses produced by these parsers are a long way from representing the full meaning of the sentences that are parsed. In particular, they do not specify "Who did What to Whom, and How, When and Where?" For computers to make effective use of information encoded in text, it is essential that they be able to detect the events that are being described and the event participants. The processing of a sentence like *John threw a ball to Mary in the park* should result in the identification of a *throwing* event involving *John* as the Agent or Causer of the event, *Mary* as the Recipient and the *ball* as the item being *thrown*. The location of the *throwing* event, or where it took place, is *the park*. This description of the event specifies the conceptual relations that the referents of the noun phrases play with respect to the verb. Our *throw* example seems fairly straightforward, but complexities quickly arise. English, for instance, allows several different syntactic constituents to present the same semantic role, and several different semantic roles to be presented by the same syntactic constituent. A central concern of linguists for decades has been the elucidation of the process of mapping from the syntactic analysis of the sentence to the underlying predicate argument structures (also known as Linking Theory).

As a simple example, in the sentences

(1) a. *John broke the window.*

   b. *The window broke.*

a standard syntactic parser will represent *the window* as the verb's direct object in the first sentence and its subject in the second. There is nothing syntactic to indicate that it has the same conceptual relation in both cases although it is expressed differently syntactically. We can capture this by annotating *the window* as having the same *semantic role* (or conceptual relation) in both sentences. It would typically be labeled as the Patient, the participant undergoing a change of state. Note that both sentences are in the active voice, as opposed to the passive voice, *The window was broken by John.* The passive provides syntactic evidence that the *window* is playing the same role (Patient) that it plays in example (1). Since the particular pair of syntactic variations illustrated with *break* does not occur with every transitive (binary) verb (see Example 2), it is not easily predictable. Other transitive verbs can also occur in intransitive (unary) form while maintaining the same semantic role for the subject that the transitive has, as in the following example where the *Sargeant* is the Agent of *play* in both sentences (*taps* would be the Theme):

(2)   a. *The sergeant played taps.*[1]

      b. *The sergeant played.*

The same verb, *play*, can also move the Theme to subject position, as in

(3) *Taps played quietly in the background.*

although other transitive verbs, such as *eat*, would not.

(4)   a. *John ate the apple.*

      b. *John ate.*

      c. **The apple ate crunchily in the background.*

The last sentence is starred (*) to indicate its ungrammaticality.

Even in transitive usages the semantic role of the verb's direct object can vary, and could be the Theme or the Instrument,

(5)   a. *The sergeant played taps.*

      b. *The sergeant played a beat-up old bugle.*

Accurate interpretation of the semantic roles of the verb arguments, i.e., "Who did What to Whom?" is a crucial goal for natural language processing systems. There has been substantial progress recently in our ability to do this automatically, based to a large degree on the availability of annotated corpora. This book first describes the motivations behind the annotations, and then it describes techniques for developing automated systems.

1.2   LINGUISTIC BACKGROUND

Ever since Fillmore's seminal paper on "deep" cases as semantically typed verb arguments (Fillmore, 1968), there has been debate over the evidence for the existence of semantic roles, how many there are, and what their categories might be. In this paper, Fillmore supported the notion of case relations (which many languages mark morphologically at the surface level), occurring initially at deep structure from which the surface-structure cases are derived. Every Noun Phrase (NP) associated with a verb is assigned a deep-structure case. The list of cases discussed in the original publication included Agentive, Instrumental, Dative, Factitive, Locative and Objective. With respect to the assignment of "deep" cases the role of grammatical object is as important as the role of grammatical subject; both are surface-structure cues to underlying case assignments. Fillmore also introduced

---

[1]Taps is a melody typically played on a bugle at the end of the day in US military institutions.

the notion of associating different types of nouns with different types of cases, e.g., the fillers of Agentive and Dative roles are most likely to be of type +ANIMATE. The number and type of roles associated with a verb are determined by the semantics of the verb itself. For example, *blush* has only a single, Dative role; *give* has three obligatory roles, the giver (the Agentive role), the thing given (the Objective role), and the recipient (the Dative role); *open* can also take three roles: the opener (Agentive), the thing opened (Objective), and an Instrument, but the Agentive and Instrument roles are optional, in contrast with *give*. Case Grammar was one of the first attempts to systematize the mapping between surface syntactic constituents and the semantic roles of the underlying predicate arguments, a linguistic endeavor that later came to be known as Linking Theory.

Fillmore proposed various linguistic tests for determining whether or not two noun phrases have the same case assignments. For instance, a conjunction test can be used as follows: only noun phrases with the same case can be conjoined. So *John and Mary broke the window* is fine, but **John and a hammer broke the window* is not. This paper had a tremendous impact on the field of linguistics, with the benefits of case theory being readily apparent. The potential for semantic generalizations was particularly appealing. If the same verb sense can have alternative role assignments that account for the differences between *Mother is cooking the potatoes/The potatoes are cooking/Mother is cooking*, then fewer types are needed for describing the lexicon. Even broader generalizations can be made, if *like* and *please* can be considered semantically equivalent, distinguished only by their preferred mappings between grammatical roles and cases. They can both be described as taking the Objective and Dative roles, but with *like,* the Subject is the *liker* (the Dative) and the Object is the *thing being liked* (the Objective) whereas with *please* the mappings are reversed, and the Subject is the *thing being liked* (the Objective) while the Object is the *liker* (the Dative). There are obvious commonalities between the Agentive cases and the Objective cases of actions such as *hitting, breaking*, and *cutting*, and surely capturing these commonalities as explicit generalizations is desirable. Where natural language processing is concerned, the immediate gains would be even more enticing. Inference rules could be written with respect to a finite set of cases rather than thousands of individual lexical items. Table 1.1 gives a list of semantic roles, or Thematic roles (also called cases and theta-roles), that are generally agreed upon (Saeed, 2003). In this table, Fillmore's Agentive role has become the Agent, the Objective is now a Patient or a Theme, and the Dative is a Recipient or a Goal.

Syntactically, a verb has a subcategorization frame which corresponds to the underlying predicate argument structure. English verbs are typically intransitive (one argument), transitive (two arguments) or ditransitive (three arguments).[2] The *Theta-grid* is the term given to the set of semantic roles, also known as Theta-roles, that are associated with the argument positions of a predicating expression such as a verb. The verb *give* from the example above is a ditransitive verb, and, using the typical role labels from Table 1.1, its Theta-grid would be [Agent, Theme, Goal]. A similar ditransitive is *put* with a Theta-grid of [Agent, Theme, Location], as in [Agent *John*] *put* [Theme *the book*] *in* [Location *his room*]. Notice that the same locative prepositional phrase that can indicate an

---

[2]But there are notable exceptions, such as *rent* which arguably can be described as having at least four roles if not five, as in *Bill rented the apartment from the agency for his cousin at $500 a month.*

	Table 1.1: A set of widely recognized Semantic Roles	
Role	**Description**	**Examples**
Agent	Initiator of action, capable of volition	**The batter** smashed the pitch into left field. **The pilot** landed the plane as lightly as a feather.
Patient	Affected by action, undergoes change of state	David trimmed **his beard**. John broke **the window**.
Theme	Entity moving, or being "located"	Paola threw **the Frisbee. The picture** hangs above the fireplace.
Experiencer	Perceives action but not in control	**He** tasted the delicate flavor of the baby lettuce. **Chris** noticed the cat slip through the partially open door.
Beneficiary	For whose benefit action is performed	He sliced **me** a large chunk of prime rib, and I could hardly wait to sit down to start in on it. The Smiths rented an apartment **for their son**.
Instrument	Intermediary/means used to perform an action	He shot the wounded buffalo with **a rifle**. The surgeon performed the incision with **a scalpel**.
Location	Place of object or action	There are some real monsters hiding **in the anxiety closet**. The band played **on the stage**.
Source	Starting point	The jet took off **from Nairobi**. We heard the rumor **from a friend**.
Goal	Ending point	The ball rolled **to the other end of the hall**. Laura lectured **to the class**.

obligatory role for a verb like *put* can also indicate a location for an event as a whole where it is considered an adjunct rather than a semantic role as in [Agent *John*] *played* [Theme *his guitar*] *in his room for hours*. The phrase *in his room* provides the location for the guitar-playing event and is a locative adjunct, similarly to *in the park* in *The children are flying kites in the park*. The phrase *for hours* is a temporal adjunct, which can also be broadly applicable. This gives us a three-way distinction between obligatory semantic roles, optional semantic roles, and adjuncts.

There can be many verbs with the same theta-grid, and these can often be formed into classes. To a large degree this is the basis for semantic classes in both VerbNet and FrameNet, as discussed in Chapter 2.

As a thought exercise, what would be the correct semantic role labels and Theta-grids for the set of sentences in Table 1.2? (See Table 1.3 for the answers.)

Table 1.2: Thought Exercise 1: Provide individual semantic role labels for each [bracketed] constituent and Theta-grids for each sentence
[The ball] flew [into the outfield.]
[Jim] gave [the book] [to the professor.]
[Laura] talked [to the class][about the bomb threats.]
[Laura] scolded [the class.]
[Bill] cut [his hair] [with a razor.]
[Gina] crashed [the car] [with a resounding boom.]

However, in spite of the intuitive appeal of case theory, the field has failed to form a consensus around a set of cases or a set of tests for determining them. There may be general agreement on the cases (or Thematic Roles or Semantic Roles) in Table 1.1 (Saeed, 2003), but there is substantial disagreement on exactly when and where they can be assigned and which additional cases should be added, if any. Thanks to some clarifications by Jackendoff, distinguishing between the Agent and the Patient (Fillmore's Objective case) is reasonably straightforward. The Agent is the initiator of the action, the doer, and can typically be described as acting deliberately or on purpose. The question *What did X do?* can be applied, with X being the Agent. The Patient, on the other hand, is being acted upon. It is likely to change state as a result of the Agent's actions. The questions *What happened to Y?* or *What did X do to Y?* would apply with Y as the Patient (Jackendoff, 1972).

It is harder to draw clear boundaries between Patients and Themes. The difference is supposed to be that Patients undergo a change of state whereas Themes simply change location. So, in *The window broke*, the *window* changes from a single pane of glass into several glass fragments and, therefore, is a Patient. On the other hand, in *The ball rolled down the hill*, the *ball* is still fundamentally the same ball at the bottom of the hill; it is simply in a different location and is, therefore, acting as a Theme. This seems straightforward enough, but other examples are more puzzling. If *the kitten licks my fingers*, have my fingers undergone a change of state or a change of location or neither? So, are the fingers a Patient or a Theme? In *The ascetic Shiva is smeared with ashes*, has the Shiva undergone a change of state or not? What about someone being *tarred and feathered*? Has that caused a more fundamental change of state in the involuntary victim than would be caused by the act of smearing oneself with ashes?

Actually, the definition of an Agent is more complicated than it might first appear as well. For instance, do Agents always have to be acting deliberately? What about the *storm* in *Earlier this year, a storm blew down a section of our fence?* Few people would ascribe intentionality to the *storm*; yet, it certainly "acted upon" the fence. Are the *the tractors* Agents in *the third tractor pushed the tight trees and stumps while the two others pulled...?* Some theories distinguish between intentionally acting Agents and non-volitional Causes, as illustrated by the Cruse reference given below.

As a second thought exercise, take any paragraph from any newspaper and try to label some part of each sentence with one or more of the roles Agent, Patient, or Theme. Since sentences usually have 2 or 3 predicate argument structures, there should be several options. Label all of the ones that are clear, but also try to make explicit your reservations about the others - why are they more problematic?

The notion of Agenthood is notoriously difficult to capture, and Cruse subdivided it into the following four subtypes (Cruse, 1973):

a. Volitive "an act of the will is stated or implied" (p. 18).

b. Effective "exerts a force...because of its position, movement, etc." (p. 19).

c. Initiative "initiation of an action by giving a command" (p. 20).

d. Agentive "performed by an object [living things, certain types of machine, and natural agents] regarded as using its own energy in carrying out the action" (p. 21).

Bill, in *Bill stabbed John*, is Volitive whereas the *glacier* in *The slow movement of the glacier gradually deepened the valley* is Effective. The *general* in *The general marched the soldiers across the parade ground* is showing Initiative, and the *car* in *The car swerved violently to the left but held the road* is Agentive. The question then remains of which, if any, Agent properties do these roles share, and how can they be determined?

There is an additional way in which semantic roles have proven to be troublesome, this time in relation to their correspondence to syntactic constituents. Chomsky defined the Theta-criterion, which stated that there should be a one-to-one correspondence between noun phrases and theta roles (Chomsky, 1982). This was met with universal acclaim. After all, what better purpose could syntactic constituents serve than to appropriately and unambiguously introduce semantic arguments? However, Jackendoff soon came up with counter-examples such as, *Esau sold his birthright to Jacob for a bowl of porridge* (Jackendoff, 1983). The standard labeling for *sell* is provided below, but notice that the *porridge* is not labeled.

(6) [Agent (or Source) *Esau*] sold [Theme *his birthright*] [Goal *to Jacob*] for a bowl of porridge.

The *porridge* would more appropriately be labeled as the Theme in a Theta-grid for the opposite transaction that has Jacob as the Source and Esau as the Goal since the *porridge* is transferred from Jacob's possession to Esau's possession, in exchange for the birthright. However, that would result in Jacob and Esau each having two different thematic role labels, one for each transaction. There are presumably other solutions to this dilemma, such as defining a complicated new Medium of Exchange role for the *porridge* as part of the *sell* Theta-grid, which would include the understanding that it goes in the opposite direction of the Theme being sold.[3] However, there are other equally problematic examples that also require special purpose solutions. The difficulty in finding satisfactory answers to these questions has revealed the inadequacy of a simple set of semantic role labels, and it has led researchers to search for radically different theoretical frameworks.

Gruber (1965) and Jackendoff have sought to provide more explanatory power by situating the original semantic roles as arguments to underlying conceptual predicates as in Jackendoff's influential theory of Lexical Conceptual Structures (Jackendoff, 1972, 1983). Dowty has backed away from a multitude of semantic role labels by persuasively defining Prototypical Agents and Patients so that each one covers a range of different semantic role types (Dowty, 1991). Levin has grouped verbs together into classes based on finding commonalities in syntactic expression, which are presumably related to the same commonalities semantic roles were intended to capture but without overtly committing to the same kinds of labels (Levin, 1993). Meanwhile, Filmore has continued exploring the space of lexical semantics, and now has a fully realized set of semantic frames for different verb types that encompasses over two thousand semantic roles, called Frame Elements (Fillmore, 1985). All of these approaches are explained in more detail below.

Table 1.3: Semantic role labels and Theta-grids for Thought Exercise 1
[Theme The ball] flew [Goal into the outfield.] [Theme, Goal]
[Agent Jim] gave [Patient the book] [Goal to the professor.] [Agent,Patient,Goal]
[Agent Laura] talked [Goal to the class][Theme about the bomb threats.] [Agent,Theme,Goal]
[Agent Laura] scolded [Patient the class.] [Agent,Patient]
[Agent Bill] cut [Patient his hair] [Instrument with a razor.] [Agent,Patient,Instrument]
[Agent Gina] crashed [Patient the car] with a resounding boom. [Agent,Patient]

1.3   MORE ELABORATED FRAMEWORKS

1.3.1   LEXICAL CONCEPTUAL STRUCTURES

Building on ideas about semantics first expounded by Gruber (1965), Jackendoff elaborated significantly on the notion of cases by treating them as arguments to a set of primitive conceptual predicates such as: GO, BE, STAY, LET, CAUSE (Jackendoff, 1972, 1983). GO can be used to describe changes of location as well as changes of possession and changes of state, any situation where both a "before state" and a different "after state" can be defined. The basic GO predicate takes three arguments, the object undergoing the change and the before and after locations, possessors, or states. For instance, *John drove from Denver to San Francisco* becomes

(7) GO (John, Denver, San Francisco)

In later versions of Lexical Conceptual Structure (LCS), the original primitives were given subtypes to provide finer granularity, as in the more elaborate version of the same sentence in Example 8.

---

[3]FrameNet has separate roles for Goods and Means in the Commerce-sell Frame.

The GO predicate is subdivided into positional (written GOposit), possessional (GOposs), and identificational (GOident) *GO*, for change of location, change of possession, and change of state, respectively. More information can be added, e.g., the manner of motion in (7) could be represented by adding a predicate: MANNER: Drivingly. An example of this detailed notation is shown in Example (8), but the simpler notation used in Example (7) will be sufficient for the rest of our discussion.

(8) [$_{event}$ GO$_{POSIT}$
    ([$_{thing}$ John],
    [$_{path}$ FROM ([$_{place}$ AT (Denver)])],
    [$_{path}$ TO ([$_{place}$ AT (San Francisco)])])
    [MANNER: Drivingly]]

By positing this underlying semantic structure for all motion verbs, Jackendoff committed to having both Source (FROM) and Goal (TO) argument positions, rather than allowing them to be optional adjuncts. This is Jackendoff's resolution of the quandary over whether or not Sources and Goals are full-fledged arguments or adjuncts. (However, for a different resolution see Dowty (2003).) They are still syntactically optional, but they always appear in the conceptual structure even when they are not mentioned explicitly. So, the representation of *The bird left the cage* has a *y* variable for the unknown destination, or Goal, of the bird. In contrast, the Goal for *put* is also included in the LCS but is syntactically obligatory, so it always has to be instantiated.

(9) GO$_{POSIT}$ (bird, cage, y)

In *John took the bird from the cage*, the event structure is more complex: we add a CAUSE predicate, which takes the Agent as the first argument and another predicate as its second argument, as in (10).

(10) CAUSE(John, [GO$_{POSIT}$ (bird, cage, y)])

Using both GO and CAUSE, we can now illustrate *give* which is quite similar to *take*, but with a possessional GO$_{POSS}$ and an explicit destination for the item being given. The three argument positions of the GO predicate have roughly the same interpretation as they do for POSIT. The first argument is the object whose POSITion or POSSessor is changing, the second argument is the POSITion or POSSESSor at the beginning of the event, and the third argument is the final POSITion or POSSESSor. *Pooh gave the honeypot to Rabbit* can be represented as below, with Pooh Causing the possession of the honeypot to GO from Pooh to Rabbit.

(11) CAUSE(Pooh, [GO$_{POSS}$ (Honeypot, Pooh, Rabbit)])

Jackendoff's intent was never to provide detailed representations of all of meaning but, instead, to focus on fundamental concepts that had special relevance to the mapping between syntax and semantics. Causation is of paramount importance in every language and is often morphologically marked. As the highest semantic predicate in which others can be embedded, it conveys a special status to the Agent role with respect to the other semantic roles. If present, the Agent will always be the Subject, also the outermost grammatical role for English. The Patient would come next, in an hierarchical ordering of the semantic roles.

In general, rather than assigning each semantic role to a particular syntactic position, Jackendoff assumes a mapping between an ordered list of semantic roles (a thematic hierarchy) and an ordered list of syntactic constituents (Jackendoff, 1992). He defines this in his principle of Hierarchical Argument Linking.

> **Hierarchical Argument Linking** (version (1) Following the thematic hierarchy, order the [semantic] roles in the LCS of a verb V from first to nth. To derive the syntactic argument structure of V, map this ordering of [semantic] roles into the first through nth roles in the syntactic hierarchy [p. 247] (Jackendoff, 1992).

Applying the same principle, the Patient can be the Subject if the Agent is not present. In the absence of the Agent, the Patient becomes the highest order argument.

The elegance and powerful generalization properties of LCS had a strong appeal for natural language processing researchers, and LCS is featured as the primary form of semantic representation for verbs in a system that solved physics problems (Palmer, 1990), one of the more successful early Message Understanding Conference (MUC) systems (Palmer et al., 1993), and as the basis for an approach to interlingual machine translation (Dorr, 1994; Dorr and Voss, 1996). However, as intuitively satisfying as the above examples are, the task of extending this approach to all of the verbs in multiple languages and, in particular, to more abstract verbs, has proved daunting.

As a third thought exercise, give the (simplified) LCS representations for the sentences in Table 1.4, before looking at the representations in Table 1.5.

Table 1.4: Thought Exercise 3: Provide LCS representations for these sentences
The ball rolled to the other end of the hall.
Jim gave the book to the professor.
Mary ejected Jim from the room.
Laura quickly whispered the latest rumour about the Queen to her cousin.
Bill cut his hair with a razor.
Gina crashed the car into the embankment.

1.3.2 PROTO-ROLES

Jackendoff's aim was to clarify the nature of individual semantic roles and their mappings to syntax by specifying the underlying conceptual predicates. Dowty took a completely different approach, borrowing from prototype theory. Psychologists, philosophers and linguists had long recognized the difficulty of defining axioms that unequivocally identify members of individual semantic categories such as *tigers*, so they had eventually resorted to defining prototypes for the categories instead (Rosch, 1973; Wittgenstein, 1953; Lakoff, 1987). Not every tiger has whiskers and gold and black stripes, lives in the jungle and hunts voraciously, but most people would recognize an animal that has those characteristics as a prototypical tiger. In the same way, Dowty posited that though every Agent may not be a sentient being that volitionally causes a change of state in another participant, we can all recognize this as a prototypical Agent, and most Agents will participate in this set of characteristics to varying degrees (Dowty, 1991). He defined a set of likely Proto-Agent Properties and Proto-Patient Properties, as described in Table 1.6.

Rather than defining a single underlying conceptual predicate that would capture the essence of agenthood, Dowty's emphasis was on associating enough defining characteristics with Agents and Patients so that it would always be possible to tell them apart. This allows the definition of principles that determine which roles are associated with which grammatical relations (or syntactic constituents) (Dowty, 1991). In any given sentence, the Agent and the Patient should be clearly distinguishable and easily assignable to the appropriate syntactic constituent: Agents to Subjects and Patients to Objects. Several of the properties are actually defined with respect to other participants, such as, *Causing an event or change of state in another participant* or *Movement (relative to position of another participant)* for Agents. For Patients, the mirror properties are *Causally affected by another participant* and *Stationary relative to movement of another participant*. Each of these properties is considered an entailment or logical implication of this participant being associated with the action or event described by the verb in this role. However, they do not all have to hold for a specific participant and a specific verb. If an event participant is acting as an Agent, then at least one of the Agent properties must be entailed or implied. If an event participant is acting as a Patient, then at least one of the Patient properties must be implied. Hence, recognizing one or more Agent properties (or Patient properties) as related to an event participant means the participant can be labeled as an Agent (or as a Patient). Dowty's Argument Selection Principle (his version of Linking Theory) for two- or three-place predicates is defined as the following:

> In predicates with grammatical subject and object, the argument for which the predicate entails the greatest number of Proto-Agent properties will be lexicalized as the subject of the predicate; the argument having the greatest number of Proto-Patient entailments will be lexicalized as the direct object. [p. 576] (Dowty, 1991).

Dowty recognized that there could be times when the number of entailments for each semantic role would be similar, and he predicted that in such cases, the likely result would be syntactic alternations, as discussed below.

Any theory of thematic roles must also include a discussion of how they map onto grammatical roles or Linking Theory. The Argument Selection Principle predicts that Agents are typically Subjects and Patients are typically Direct Objects, but it does not have predictions for third or even fourth arguments. However, many verbs have more than two arguments, so other roles need to be taken into consideration. The third argument of a ditransitive verb is typically labeled as the

---

Table 1.5: LCS representations for Thought Exercise 3 sentences

The ball rolled to the other end of the hall.
GO_{POSIT}(ball, x, end-of-hall)
Jim gave the book to the professor.
CAUSE(Jim, [GO_{POSS} (book, Jim, professor)])
Mary ejected Jim from the room.
CAUSE(Mary, [GO_{POSIT} (Jim, room, y)])
Laura quickly whispered the latest rumour about the Queen to her cousin.
CAUSE(Laura, [$GO_{?}$(rumour, Laura, cousin)]), MANNER(whisperingly)
Bill cut his hair with a razor.
CAUSE(Bill, [GO_{IDENT}(hair, x, cut)])
Gina crashed the car into the embankment.
CAUSE(Gina, [GO_{POSIT}(car, x, embankment)])

Table 1.6: Dowty's properties of Proto-roles

Proto-Agent Properties:
Volitional involvement in event or state
Sentience (and/or perception)
Causing an event or change of state in another participant
Movement (relative to position of another participant)
(exists independently of event named)
Agent, also Experiencer, Instrument, Actor, Causer, etc.

Proto-Patient Properties:
Undergoes change of state
Incremental theme
Causally affected by another participant
Stationary relative to movement of another participant
(does not exist independently of the event, or at all
Patient, also Theme, Percepts, etc.

Oblique argument. Dowty also offers us the following Thematic Role Hierarchy which states that Instruments and Benefactives have the same precedence as Agents, and Patients take precedence over Sources and Goals:

```
Agent/Instrument/Benefactive > Patient > Source/Goal
```

An important deviation from the widely accepted semantic role definitions listed in Table 1.1 is the labeling of the Object in Motion (movement relative to position of another participant) as an Agent rather than a Theme. Instead of labeling objects in motion as Themes, Dowty introduces the notion of an Incremental Theme, an important argument that is diminished or increased during the course of an event, helping to determine the event's culmination. This provides a particularly compelling explanation for the slight differences in meaning associated with the *spray/load* alternation as discussed in the paragraph below on Incremental Themes.

Incremental Themes   A well known syntactic alternation is the *spray/load* alternation, which might seem to be a likely candidate for a competition between potential Proto-Patients. In the following examples, the Direct Object alternates between the Patient being *loaded* or *sprayed* and its intended Goal:

(12)   a. Mary loaded the hay onto the truck.

      b. Mary loaded the truck with hay.

      c. Mary sprayed the paint onto the wall.

      d. Mary sprayed the wall with paint.

These examples are generally accepted as having a subtle shift in meaning, and linguists and lexicographers have debated over whether or not they actually represent distinct entries of both *spray* and *load*. In Example (12a), the implication is that all of the hay ends up on the truck, but the truck may or may not be full. In Example (12b), the implication is that the truck is completely full of hay, but there may be additional hay that has not yet been loaded anywhere. By introducing the Incremental Theme role, Dowty provides an elegant explanation. An Incremental Theme is an event participant that is undergoing a change of state and the completion of the change of state signals the termination of the event. If the Incremental Theme is the hay, the change of state is its change of location to the truck. If the truck is the Incremental Theme, it is changing state from being empty to being filled. In either case, the event only terminates when all of the hay is moved or when the truck is completely filled. According to Dowty, it is the shift from one type of Incremental Theme to another that accounts for the difference in meaning, but the same sense of the verb is being referenced.

Example Sentences   The LCS examples from the previous section are all repeated in Table 1.7, with notes as to the salient Agent or Patient properties. With the exception of *give* (the thing given is considered to have more Proto-Patient properties than the Recipient), these are all fairly straightforward but, as discussed below, the distinctions can sometimes be quite subtle.

Competing candidates for Proto-roles   We have already seen with the 3-place predicate *give* that a choice had to be made between two possible candidates for the Proto-patient role label, the Theme and the Recipient. The Theme can be considered to be more causally affected than the Recipient, and thus it can be labeled as the Patient. Both the ditransitive form and the dative alternation for *give* have the *thing given* as the Direct Object, so the alternations are labeled consistently, with the

Table 1.7: Examples of the use of Dowty's Proto-roles
[Agent The ball] rolled [Goal to the other end of the hall]. *Agent-Movement (relative to position of another participant)* [Agent Jim] gave [Patient the book] [Goal to the professor]. *Agent-Volitional, Sentient, Causer; Patient-Undergoes change of state (change of owner)* [Agent Mary] ejected [Patient Jim] from the room. *Agent-Volitional, Sentient, Causer; Patient-Causally affected* [Agent Laura] quickly whispered [Patient the latest rumour about the Queen] [Goal to her cousin]. *Agent-Volitional, Sentient, Causer; Patient* [Agent Bill] cut [IncrTheme his hair] [Instrument with a razor]. *Agent-Volitional, Sentient, Causer; Incremental Theme* [Agent Gina] crashed [Patient the car] [Goal into the embankment]. *Agent-Volitional, Sentient, Causer; Patient-Causally affected*

Recipient always as the Oblique (Indirect Object or Prepositional Phrase). Using Dowty's thematic role hierarchy, the Recipient would eventually receive a Benefactive label.

Psychological predicates, or *psych* verbs, nouns, and adjectives, provide another interesting example, illustrated here with verbs. There are several pairs of verbs in English that have a similar semantics with a shift in perspective, as illustrated in Table 1.8. Dowty distinguishes them as having either Experiencer (sentient) Subjects that participate in the emotion or mental process being described or Stimulus (causers of an emotional reaction) Subjects, either of which could be a Proto-Agent (Dowty, 1991).

Table 1.8: Examples of Dowty's Psychological Predicates, p. 579	
Experiencer Subject	**Stimulus Subject**
x likes y	y pleases x
x fears y	y frightens x
x supposes (that) S	(it) seems (to) x (that) S
x regards y (as) VP	y strikes x (as) VP
x is surprised at y	y surprises x
x is disturbed at y	y disturbs x

Since both *x* and *y* have the same number of entailments (properties) which could result in them being labeled as Agents, and hence appearing as Subjects, how is the shift in perspective achieved? With the Stimulus Subject verbs, supposedly there is a stronger implication that during the event the Experiencer undergoes a change of state which results in the emotional state being described. This counts as being causally affected by the Stimulus. Therefore, for *please* and *frighten* the Experiencer has the most number of Patient role entailments, making it the Direct Object and leaving the Subject position open for the Stimulus Subject. In the Experiencer Subject verbs, the assumption is that the Experiencer's reaction being described is a known, continuing state; hence, no change of state is involved and the Experiencer is the Subject.

As we have already discussed, many different types of semantic roles can fit Dowty's definition of a Proto-Agent. The examples in Table 1.9 illustrate the wide range. By the same token, Proto-Patients can also cover a wide range, as illustrated by Table 1.10. As a thought exercise, go through the examples in Table 1.1 and label each role as a Proto-Agent, a Proto-Patient or an Oblique. Dowty's theory offers a powerful mechanism for recognizing properties that are shared among various roles without stripping away their uniqueness.

Table 1.9: Examples of Prototypical Agents	
Traditional Thematic Role Label	Example
Agent	The batter hit the ball.
Experiencer	I forgot to pay my taxes.
Instrument	The stock market plunge opened Congress's pockets.

Table 1.10: Examples of Prototypical Patients	
Traditional Thematic Role Label	Example
Patient	Queen Victoria's composure never cracks. The Chautauqua movement eventually died.
Theme	The stock market plunged dramatically. Congress flew to the rescue.
Recipient	Mary received a Valentine's card from John.
Recipient	The GOP suffered from the economic woes.

1.3.3   LEVIN'S *VERB CLASSES AND ALTERNATIONS*

Dowty was focused on leveraging commonalities among roles. In her comprehensive and meticulous comparison of the syntactic behavior of over 3000 verbs, Levin, in contrast, focused on subtle distinctions (Levin, 1993). Levin argues that syntactic variations are a direct reflection of the underlying semantics; the set of syntactic frames associated with a particular verb reflect underlying semantic components, that constrain allowable arguments. On this principle, Levin defines verb classes based on the ability of each verb to occur or not occur in pairs of syntactic frames that are in some sense meaning preserving (diathesis alternations). Therefore, the members of a class must share one or more semantic components which can be preserved in the same way. For example, the *break* sentences in Example (1), repeated here, are related by a transitive/intransitive alternation called the causative/inchoative alternation where the transitive is the *causative*, a change of state with an explicit mention of an Agent and the intransitive is the *inchoative*, describing solely the change of state without reference to the causer.

(13) a. *John broke the window.*

   b. *The window broke.*

Break, and verbs such as *shatter* and *smash*, are also characterized by their ability to appear in the middle construction, as in

(14) *Glass breaks/shatters/smashes easily.*[4]

Cut, a similar change-of-state verb, seems to share in this syntactic behavior, and can also appear in the transitive (causative) as well as the middle construction,

(15) a. *John cut the bread.*

   b. *This loaf cuts easily.*

However, it cannot also occur in the simple intransitive, so it does not participate in the causative/inchoative alternation.

(16) a. *The window broke.*

   b. **The bread cut.*

In contrast, *cut* verbs can occur in another construction called the *conative* whereas *break* verbs cannot. The conative indicates a recognizable action being performed that is trying for a goal which may not be achieved.

(17) a. *John valiantly cut/hacked at the frozen loaf, but his knife was too dull to make a dent in it.*

   b. **John broke at the window.*

   The explanation given is that *cut* describes a series of actions directed at achieving the goal of separating some object into pieces. These actions consist of grasping an instrument with a sharp edge such as a knife and applying it in a cutting fashion to the object. When *cutting bread with a knife* the action might be described as directed-motion; if a *carpenter is cutting wood with a bandsaw*, the action might be described quite differently. However, there is still an action that corresponds directly with the *cut* being achieved as opposed to *break* which has no specific associated action.

---

[4]Note that the *Taps played quietly in the background* is also in the middle construction.

It is also possible for these *cutting* actions to be performed without the end result being achieved but where the cutting manner can still be recognized, as in the conative, *John cut at the rope*. Where *break* is concerned, the only thing specified is the resulting change of state where the object becomes separated into pieces, so there is no recognizable action that could be independent of the resulting state. However, a simple description of the resulting state as in *The window broke* is coherent. With *cut*, the Agent is a necessary enough participant in the action that it must be invoked, either explicitly, as in the transitive, or implicitly, as in the middle construction. If the *cutting* was *easy*, it must have been *easy* for someone. A simple statement of the resulting state without any reference to the action, *The bread cut* is not coherent.

Relying on this type of syntactic analysis, Levin organizes 3100 verbs, many of which have multiple senses, into 47 top level classes. The classes are further subdivided into dozens of smaller, more specific classes. Several classes with their members and some characteristic alternations are given in Table 1.11. The same classes with the suggested underlying semantic components that are reflected in the syntactic alternations are given in Table 1.12. As with many of these semantic frameworks, the goal is not to attempt a complete specification of meaning but rather to pinpoint specific semantic elements that interact during the mapping between syntax and semantics.

This verb classification is something of an outlier in our description of semantic theories since it does not provide explicit semantic role labels. They are referred to implicitly by the very nature of the diathesis alternations, which are defined as "meaning preserving." The alternation in question is typically the movement of a particular semantic role from one syntactic constituent to another as in the movement of the Patient from Object to Subject in the causative/inchoative alternation. However, there is no actual labeling of the *window* as a Patient in the *break* class. In particular, there is no assertion that the Agent of a *cutting* action might have anything in common with the Agent of a *breaking* action.

Table 1.11: Some example Levin classes		
Class	**Syntactic Frames**	**Members**
break 45.1	John broke the jar. / The jar broke. / Jars break easily.	*break, chip, crack, crash, crush, fracture, rip, shatter, smash, snap, splinter, snip, tear*
cut 21.1	John cut the bread. / *The bread cut. / Bread cuts easily.	*chip, chop, clip, cut, hack, hew, rip, saw, scrape, scratch, slash, slice, snip*
hit 18.1	John hit the wall. / *The wall hit. / *Walls hit easily.	*bang, bash, click, dash, squash, tamp, thump, thwack, whack, batter, beat, bump, butt, drum, hammer, hit, jab, kick, knock, lash, pound, rap, slap, smack, smash, strike, tap*

Table 1.12: The same classes with semantic components

Class	Syntactic Frames	Semantic Components
break 45.1	John broke the jar. / The jar broke. / Jars break easily.	**change-of-state**
cut 21.1	John cut the bread. / *The bread cut. / Bread cuts easily.	**change-of-state, recognizable action, sharp instrument**
hit 18.1	John hit the wall. / *The wall hit. / *Walls hit easily.	**contact, exertion of force**

The idea of a close mapping between possible syntactic variations of a verb and its underlying semantics is intuitively appealing. Theoretically, a distributional analysis of enough grammatical sentences could be used to assign a previously unseen verb to a class, whereupon it could be associated with the semantic components that characterize that class. However, the verb classes as currently specified do not lend themselves readily to this type of exercise.

First, there are practical problems, such as lemma coverage and sense coverage. Even with 3100 verbs, the lemma coverage is limited. Only half of the 3000 verb lemmas in the Penn Treebank, a one million word corpus of Wall Street Journal articles, are included in the classes. WordNet has well over 8000 verb lemmas. For the verbs that are present, although one or two basic senses are usually covered, it is rare to find the entire range of senses that might be found in a standard dictionary. Since different senses of a verb can be in different classes with distinct sets of syntactic frames, any distributional analysis based on syntactic behavior must be able to appropriately segregate syntactic frames according to sense. If all of the syntactic frames for several senses of the same verb are jumbled together, there will be no clear association with any particular class. Accurate sense tagging is, therefore, a prerequisite to successful clustering based on syntactic frames.

There are also issues related to the theoretical status of the syntactic frames associated with each class. Even for verbs that are only in a single class, class assignment based on a simple distributional analysis might assume that the entire range of frames for a particular class will appear at least once or twice for every verb in the class. However, this rarely happens in a single corpus or even in a large document collection, partly because of random chance and partly because of common usage. Close perusal of the class and frame definitions indicates that some members of a class are much more likely to appear in certain frames than other members. For instance, *wash* is in the *Prepare* class with many other verbs describing household tasks such as *grilling, poaching, pouring, cleaning, etc.* This class includes the ditransitive and double-object frames, *She grilled a steak for me/She grilled me a steak.* Whereas, *She washed a shirt for me* is very common, Google has exactly one instance of *She washed me a shirt* from a 1914 WWI letter. Double object constructions are much more natural with the cooking verbs in this class than with the other verbs although not technically ungrammatical with any of them.

There can also be a large overlap in the sets of syntactic frames characterizing two or more classes, with barely discernible differences. Adding even more complexity, the same verb can appear in two different classes with contradictory sets of syntactic frames. For instance, *carry* verbs are described as not taking the conative, **The mother carried at the baby*, and yet many of the verbs in the *carry* class *(push, pull, tug, shove, kick, yank)* are also listed in the *push/pull* class, which does take the conative, *He kicked at the ball*. This listing of a verb in more than one class (many verbs are in three or even four classes) is left open to interpretation. It can indicate that more than one sense of the verb is involved, in which case they might be homonyms (completely unrelated senses, such as *draw a picture* versus *draw water from the well*) or polysemes (related senses). If related, is one sense more general purpose with the others being systematic extensions of this more general one? In which case, do the alternations for the more general class take precedence over the alternations for the other classes in which the verb is listed? The issues of multiple class memberships have been explored more fully by Dang et al. (1998) and Kipper et al. (2000). Clearly there are subtle implications to verb class membership that need to be carefully weighed and balanced before we will be able to realize the full potential of this promising approach. In the meanwhile, several creative approaches for automatically inducing verb frames and verb classes have been tried with varying degrees of success (Schulte im Walde, 2009), and the original classes have been extended and made available on-line in VerbNet, as discussed in Section 2.2.

1.3.4   FRAME SEMANTICS

This introduction to linguistic theories about semantic representations ends where it began, with Charles Fillmore. Having thought deeply about the limitations of case theory and building on the notion of Frames as used for Knowledge Representation in Artificial Intelligence (Minsky, 1975), Fillmore made substantial modifications to the original theory. The original "case assignments," or semantic role labels, always made reference to a hearer's knowledge of richer, underlying semantic representations. Just as Jackendoff has the goal of making explicit the CAUSE relation in which an Agent participated, Fillmore also chooses to make more explicit the details of the event being described by a verb. But whereas Jackendoff's aim is a decompositional analysis that captures only broad generalizations with as small a set of predicates as possible, Fillmore's aim is quite different. Fillmore also makes the overarching relations between the semantic roles and the verb more explicit, and he defines them as semantic frames but without restricting himself to a small vocabulary of primitives. His goal is the elaboration of the richness and diversity of semantic relations of individual lexemes, and he is willing to specify a unique semantic frame for an individual verb if that is necessary to clarify the nature of its arguments. This theory is called Frame Semantics (Fillmore, 1985, 1982; Fillmore et al., 2002) and is embodied in FrameNet, a lexical resource which currently has entries for 10,000 lexical units (senses of a lemma) associated with at least 958 distinct frames and 2,500 Frame Elements. Annotated example sentences have been provided for up to 6800 lexical units (Baker et al., 1998; Johnson et al., 2001). FrameNet is described in more detail in the next chapter.

EXERCISES

1. Adding Semantic Role Labels

   Using the set of labels in Table 1.1 provide specific labels and Theta-grids for at least 10 clauses from one of the following paragraphs:

   The family of Dashwood had long been settled in Sussex. Their estate was large, and their residence was at Norland Park, in the centre of their property, where, for many generations, they had lived in so respectable a manner as to engage the general good opinion of their surrounding acquaintance. The late owner of this estate was a single man, who lived to a very advanced age, and who, for many years of his life, had a constant companion and housekeeper in his sister. But her death, which happened ten years before his own, produced a great alteration in his home; for to supply her loss, he invited and received into his house the family of his nephew Mr. Henry Dashwood, the legal inheritor of the Norland estate, and the person to whom he intended to bequeath it. In the society of his nephew and niece, and their children, the old gentleman's days were comfortably spent. His attachment to them all increased. The constant attention of Mr. and Mrs. Henry Dashwood to his wishes, which proceeded not merely from interest, but from goodness of heart, gave him every degree of solid comfort which his age could receive; and the cheerfulness of the children added a relish to his existence. [Jane Austen, Sense and Sensibility, P. 1]

   It was a feature peculiar to the colonial wars of North America, that the toils and dangers of the wilderness were to be encountered before the adverse hosts could meet. A wide and apparently an impervious boundary of forests severed the possessions of the hostile provinces of France and England. The hardy colonist, and the trained European who fought at his side, frequently expended months in struggling against the rapids of the streams, or in effecting the rugged passes of the mountains, in quest of an opportunity to exhibit their courage in a more martial conflict. But, emulating the patience and self-denial of the practiced native warriors, they learned to overcome every difficulty; and it would seem that, in time, there was no recess of the woods so dark, nor any secret place so lovely, that it might claim exemption from the inroads of those who had pledged their blood to satiate their vengeance, or to uphold the cold and selfish policy of the distant monarchs of Europe. [James Fenimore Cooper, The Last of the Mohicans, P. 1]

2. Now provide Lexical Conceptual Structures for the same clauses.

3. Add Dowty's Proto-Agent and Proto-Patient role labels. Did you come across any Incremental Themes?

CHAPTER 2

Available Lexical Resources

Currently, there are three English lexical resources which provide explicit semantic role labels for use in data annotation; FrameNet, VerbNet, and PropBank.[1] Resources for other languages are described in more detail in Chapter 4. The English resources have been created independently, with differing goals, and yet are surprisingly compatible. They differ primarily in the granularity of the semantic role labels. PropBank uses very generic labels such as *Arg0*, as in:

(18) [Arg0 President Bush] has [REL approved] [Arg1 duty-free treatment for imports of certain types of watches.]

In addition to providing several alternative syntactic frames and a set of semantic predicates, VerbNet marks the PropBank *Arg0* as an Agent and the *Arg1* as a Theme. FrameNet labels them as Grantor and Action, respectively, and puts them in the Grant_Permission class. The additional semantic richness provided by VerbNet and FrameNet does not contradict PropBank, but can be seen as complementary. Each of these resources is discussed below, beginning with the most fine-grained one, FrameNet.

2.1 FRAMENET

Based on Filmore's Frame Semantics, each semantic frame in FrameNet is defined with respect to its Frame Elements, which are fine-grained semantic role labels. For instance, the Frame Elements for the Apply-heat Frame include a Cook, Food, and a Heating Instrument. More traditional labels (see Table 1.1) for the same roles might be Agent, Theme, and Instrument. Members of the Apply-heat frame include *bake, barbecue, blanch, boil, braise, broil, brown*, etc. The Apply-heat lexical units all seem to be verbs, but a frame can also have adjectives and nouns such as nominalizations as members.[2] As mentioned above, the 958 individual frames are associated with well over 2,500 Frame Elements (Baker et al., 1998; Johnson et al., 2001)[3].

The Frame Elements for an individual Frame are classified in terms of how central they are, with three levels being distinguished: core (conceptually necessary for the Frame, roughly similar to syntactically obligatory), peripheral (not central to the frame, but providing additional information

---

[1]NomBank, as a companion to PropBank, provides corresponding semantic role labels for noun predicates (Meyers et al., 2004).

[2]Many of the nouns are related to verbs, like Achieving-first.invention.n, Assessing.evaluation.n, and Awareness.comprehension, but many are not, like Make-agreement-on-action.treaty.n, Natural-features.valley.n, and Part-inner-outer.exterior.n - contributed by an anonymous reviewer.

[3]Frame elements are given frame-specific names wherever possible, but there can be two distinct FEs in two different frames with the same name–or to put it differently, FE names are only unique within frames.

that situates the event, such as time and place; roughly similar to adjuncts) and extra-thematic (not specific to the frame and not standard adjuncts but situating the frame with respect to a broader context). Lexical items are grouped together based solely on having the same frame semantics, without consideration of similarity of syntactic behavior, unlike Levin's verb classes. Sets of verbs with similar syntactic behavior may appear in multiple frames, and a single FrameNet frame may contain sets of verbs with related senses but different subcategorization properties. FrameNet places a primary emphasis on providing rich, idiosyncratic descriptions of semantic properties of lexical units in context, and making explicit subtle differences in meaning.

In spite of the different motivations, there are still many overlaps between verbs in the same Levin class and verbs associated with the same FrameNet frame. For instance, the Levin *Cooking 45.3* class contains all of the FrameNet Apply-heat verbs, except for *singe*. It also includes a few additional, fairly infrequent verbs, many of which have to do with frying, such as *french-fry, oven-fry, oven-poach, overcook, overheat, pan-broil, pan-fry*, as well as a few truly rare gems such as *parch, rissole, scallop*, and *schirr*. As would be expected, the most overlap between FrameNet is with the Levin classes that are more semantically coherent. Of course, some Levin classes, such as *Braid 41.2.3: bob, braid, brush, clip, coldcream, comb, condition, crimp, crop, curl*, etc. are clearly not intended to be semantically coherent, and they have much less overlap with any FrameNet Frame. The similarities and differences between Levin's classes and FrameNet are explored in more detail by Baker and Ruppenhofer (2002).

2.2   VERBNET

VerbNet (Dang et al., 1998; Kipper et al., 2000; Kipper Schuler, 2005; Kipper et al., 2008) is midway between PropBank and FrameNet in terms of lexical specificity, and it is closer to PropBank in its close ties to syntactic structure. It consists of hierarchically arranged verb classes, inspired by and extended from the Levin classes described in Section 1.3.3. The Levin classes have 240 classes, with 47 top level classes and 193 second and third level. VerbNet has added almost 1000 lemmas as well as over 200 more classes. There is now a 4th level of classes and several additional classes at the other 3 levels. VerbNet adds to each Levin class an abstract representation of the syntactic frames with explicit correspondences between syntactic positions and the semantic roles they express as in *Agent REL Patient*, or *Patient REL into pieces* for *break*. (For other extensions of Levin see also Dorr and Jones (2000); Korhonen, Krymolowski, and Marx (2003)). The original Levin classes constitute the first few levels in the hierarchy, with each class subsequently refined to account for further semantic and syntactic differences within a class. In many cases, the additional information that VerbNet provides for each class has caused it to subdivide, or use intersections of, Levin classes.

Each class and subclass is characterized extensionally by its set of verbs and, intensionally, by a list of the arguments of those verbs and syntactic and semantic information about them. The argument list consists of semantic roles (24 in total: Agent, Patient, Theme, Experiencer, etc.[4]) and possible selectional restrictions on the arguments that are expressed using binary predicates. The semantic predicates describe the participants during various stages of the event expressed by

---

[4]For the complete list see http://verbs.colorado.edu/~mpalmer/projects/verbnet.html.

the syntactic frame and provide class-specific interpretations of the semantic roles. VerbNet now covers 3,965 verb lexemes with 471 classes. There are explicit links to similar entries in WordNet, OntoNotes groupings, FrameNet, and PropBank. A primary emphasis for VerbNet is the coherent syntactic and semantic characterization of the classes, which will facilitate the acquisition of new class members based on observable syntactic and semantic behavior.

Syntactic Frames   Each VerbNet class contains a set of syntactic descriptions, or syntactic frames, depicting the possible surface realizations of the argument structure. These include constructions such as transitive, intransitive, prepositional phrases, resultatives, and a large set of diathesis alternations listed by Levin as part of each verb class. Each syntactic frame consists of semantic roles (such as Agent, Theme, and Location), the verb, and other lexical items which may be required for a particular construction or alternation. Semantic restrictions (such as ANIMATE, HUMAN, and ORGANIZATION) are used to constrain the types of semantic roles allowed in the classes. The 36 semantic types are taken originally from the EuroWordNet Interlingua, and they can be viewed on the web.[5] They typically encompass literal meanings rather than metaphorical ones and should be thought of as preferences rather than as hard constraints. Each syntactic frame may also be constrained in terms of which prepositions are allowed. Additionally, further restrictions may be imposed on semantic roles to indicate the syntactic nature of the constituent likely to be associated with it. Levin classes are characterized primarily by Noun Phrase and Prepositional Phrase complements. Several additional classes based on work by Korhonen and Briscoe (2004) have been added to the original Levin classes, and many of these also include sentential complements. They refer only to the distinction between finite and nonfinite clauses as in the various subclasses of Verbs of Communication.

Semantic Predicates   Semantic predicates which denote the relations between participants and events are used to convey the key components of meaning for each class in VerbNet. The semantic information for the verbs in VerbNet is expressed as a conjunction of semantic predicates, such as MOTION, CONTACT or CAUSE. As the classes may be distinguished by their temporal characteristics (e.g., Verbs of *Assuming a Position* vs. Verbs of *Spatial Configuration*), it is also necessary to convey information about when each of the predicates applies. In order to capture this information, semantic predicates are associated with an event variable, e, and often with START(e), END(e) or DURING(e) arguments to indicate that the semantic predicate is in force either at the START, the END, or DURING the related time period for the entire event. The example in Figure 2.1 illustrates the information associated with an individual class, the *Pour 9.5* class, with class members, semantic role labels, syntactic frames and semantic predicates. Version 3.0 of VerbNet has 94 distinct semantic predicates, and an effort is currently underway to link the verb classes to the Omega ontology (Philpot et al., 2005) and to create upper level nodes (Palmer et al., 2009).

---

[5] http://verbs.colorado.edu/~mpalmer/projects/verbnet.html

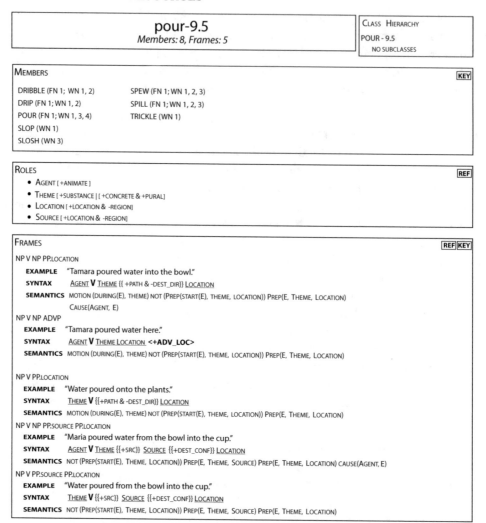

Figure 2.1: VerbNet entry for pour class

2.3   PROPBANK

In contrast with FrameNet and VerbNet, the primary goal in developing the Proposition Bank, or PropBank, was not lexical resource creation, but the development of an annotated corpus to be used as training data for supervised machine learning systems. The first PropBank release consists of 1M words of the Wall Street Journal portion of the Penn Treebank II with predicate-argument structures for verbs, using semantic role labels for each verb argument. Although the semantic role labels are purposely chosen to be quite generic and theory neutral, *Arg0*, *Arg1*, etc., they are still intended to consistently annotate the same semantic role across syntactic variations. So the *Arg1* or Patient in *John broke the window* is the same window that is annotated as the *Arg1* in *The window broke* even though it is the syntactic subject in one sentence and the syntactic object in the other. The primary goal of PropBank is to supply consistent, simple, general purpose labeling of semantic roles for a large quantity of coherent text to support the training of automatic semantic role labelers, in the same way the Penn Treebank has supported the training of statistical syntactic parsers. PropBank also provides a lexicon which lists, for each broad meaning of each annotated verb, its "Frameset," i.e., the possible arguments in the predicate and their labels (its "roleset") and all possible syntactic realizations. This lexical resource is used as a set of verb-specific guidelines by the annotators and can be seen as quite similar in nature to FrameNet and VerbNet although at a more coarse-grained level. However, PropBank is more focused on literal meaning than FrameNet is, and it pays less attention to clearly marking metaphorical usages and support verb constructions (Ellsworth et al., 2004).

Because of the difficulty of defining a universal set of semantic or thematic roles covering all types of predicates, PropBank defines semantic roles on a verb by verb basis. An individual verb's semantic arguments are numbered, beginning with 0. For a particular verb, *Arg0* is generally the argument exhibiting features of a prototypical Agent (Dowty, 1991) while *Arg1* is a prototypical Patient or Theme. No consistent generalizations can be made across verbs for the higher numbered arguments, though an effort was made to consistently define roles across members of VerbNet classes. In addition to verb-specific numbered roles, PropBank defines several more general *ArgM* (Argument Modifier) roles that can apply to any verb, and which are similar to adjuncts. These include LOCation, EXTent, ADVerbial, CAUse, TeMPoral, MaNneR, and DIRection, among others.

A set of roles or a roleset corresponds to a distinct usage of a verb. It is associated with a set of syntactic frames indicating allowable syntactic variations in the expression of that set of roles, the Frameset. A polysemous verb may have more than one Frameset when the differences in meaning are distinct enough to require different sets of roles, one set for each Frameset. The tagging guidelines include a verb-specific descriptor field for each role, such as *baker* for *Arg0* and *creation* for *Arg1* in the example below. These are intended for use during annotation and as documentation, but they do not have any theoretical standing. The collection of Frameset entries for a verb is referred to as a *Frame File*. The neutral, generic labels facilitate mapping between PropBank and other more fine-grained resources such VerbNet and FrameNet, as well as Lexical-Conceptual Structure or Prague Tectogrammatics (Rambow et al., 2003). While most rolesets have two to four numbered roles, as many as six can appear, in particular for certain verbs of motion. For more details, see Palmer et al. (2005) and the on-line Frame Files.[6]

---

[6]http://verbs.colorado.edu/framesets/

- Roleset bake.01 Verbnet Class: 1 "create via heat":

- Roles:

    - *Arg0*:baker
    - *Arg1*:creation
    - *Arg2*:source
    - *Arg3*:benefactive

(19) [$_{\text{ArgM:TMP}}$ Today] [$_{\text{Arg2}}$ whole grains] are freshly ground every day and [$_{\text{REL}}$ baked] [$_{\text{Arg1}}$ into bread].

In spite of its success in facilitating the training of semantic role labeling (SRL), there are several ways in which PropBank could be more effective, as discussed below. PropBank lacks much of the information that is contained in VerbNet, including information about selectional restrictions, verb semantics, and inter-verb relationships. We have, therefore, created a mapping between VerbNet and PropBank, and between VerbNet and FrameNet, which will allow us to use the machine learning techniques that have been developed for PropBank annotations to generate more semantically abstract VerbNet and FrameNet representations, as discussed in Section 2.4.

2.3.1   LIMITATIONS TO A VERB-SPECIFIC APPROACH

The early part of Chapter 1 described the lack of consensus in the community as to a specific set of semantic role labels. PropBank avoids this issue by using theory-agnostic labels (*Arg0, Arg1, . . . , Arg5*), and by defining those labels to have verb-specific meanings. Under this scheme, PropBank can avoid making any claims about how any one verb's arguments relate to other verbs' arguments or about general distinctions between verb arguments and adjuncts. However, there are several limitations to this approach. The first is that it can be difficult to make inferences and generalizations based on role labels that are only meaningful with respect to a single verb. Since each role label is verb-specific, we can not confidently determine when two verbs' arguments have the same role; and since no encoded meaning is associated with each tag, we cannot make generalizations across verb classes. In contrast, the use of a shared set of role labels, as in VerbNet, facilitates both inferencing and generalization.

An additional issue with PropBank's verb-specific approach is that it can make training automatic semantic role labeling (SRL) systems more difficult. Similarly, to FrameNet, a vast amount of data would be needed to train the verb-specific (or frame-specific) models that are theoretically mandated by the fine-grained role labels. Researchers using PropBank as training data for the most part ignore the "verb-specific" nature of the labels, and instead build a single model for each numbered argument (*Arg0, Arg1, . . . , Arg5*). Given the correspondence between *Arg0/Arg1* and Dowty's Proto-Agent/Proto-Patient, and the fact that they constitute 85% of the arguments, it is not surprising that this is effective. The *ArgM*'s are also labeled quite consistently. However, arguments *Arg2-Arg5* are highly overloaded, and performance drops significantly on them.

A final limitation arises from the genre-specific nature of the training corpus, which was initially entirely Wall Street Journal articles. This has since been expanded under DARPA-GALE funding to include Broadcast News, Broadcast Conversation, Newsgroups, and Weblogs, yet significant additional quantities of corpora would be needed to train a truly robust system. This issue is reflected in the relatively poor performance of most state-of-the-art SRL systems when tested on a novel genre, the Brown corpus, during CoNLL 2005. For example, the SRL system described in (Pradhan et al., 2005b; Pradhan et al., 2005a) achieves an F-score of 81% when tested on the same genre as it is trained on (WSJ); but that score drops to 68.5% when the same system is tested on a different genre (the Brown corpus). In addition to the new DARPA-GALE genres, better techniques for generalizing the semantic role labeling task are still needed. It would also be advantageous to be able to merge the FrameNet and PropBank labeled instances to create a much larger, more diverse, and yet still coherent training corpus.

Table 2.1 provides an overview of the current status of the three resources that have been discussed.

Table 2.1: A comparison of current lexical resources: FrameNet, VerbNet and PropBank			
Attribute	**FrameNet**	**VerbNet**	**PropBank**
Lexical Units (senses)	11,600	5,733	6,204
Lexemes (lemmas)	6,000	3,965 (verbs)	5,213 (verbs)
categories	960 Frames	471 Classes	
Semantic Roles	2,500+ Frame Elements	24 Thematic Role types	16 Args, 6000+ (verb specific roles)
Annotated Data	150,000 sentences covering 6,800 lexical units	1M word WSJ Treebank (90% token coverage)	1.75M word WSJ/BN/BC, etc. (all verbs)

2.4 SEMLINK

With the dual goals of being able to merge PropBank and FrameNet training data as well as being able to map back and forth between PropBank, VerbNet and FrameNet labelings for annotated instances, type to type mappings between PropBank and VerbNet have been made, as well as between VerbNet and FrameNet. These mappings have been used to leverage a mapping of the PropBank annotated instances to the relevant VerbNet classes and semantic role labels. Efforts to extend this instance mapping to FrameNet are underway. This project is called Semlink.

VerbNet-PropBank   The mapping between VerbNet and PropBank consists of two parts: a lexical mapping and an annotated corpus. The lexical mapping is responsible for specifying the potential mappings between PropBank and VerbNet for a given word; but it does not specify which of those mappings should be used for any given occurrence of the word. That is the job of the annotated corpus, which for any given instance gives the specific VerbNet mapping and semantic role labels. This can be thought of as a form of sense tagging. Where a PropBank frame maps to several VerbNet classes, they can be thought of as more fine-grained senses, and labeling with the class label corresponds to providing a sense tag label.

The lexical mapping was used to automatically predict VerbNet classes and role labels for each instance. Where the resulting mapping was one-to-many, the correct mapping was selected manually (Loper et al., 2007). The usefulness of this mapping for improving SRL on new genres is discussed in the next chapter.

VerbNet-FrameNet   The SemLink VerbNet/FrameNet mapping consists of three parts. The first part is a many-to-many mapping of VerbNet Classes and FrameNet Frames. It is many-to-many in that a given FrameNet lexical unit can map to more than one VerbNet member, and more frequently, a given VerbNet member can map to more than one FrameNet Frame. The second part is a mapping of VerbNet Semantic Roles and FrameNet Frame Elements for specific verb senses. These two parts have been provided in separate files in order to offer the cleanest possible formatting. The third part is the PropBank corpus with mappings from PropBank Frameset ID's to FrameNet Frames and mappings from the PropBank arguments to FrameNet Frame Elements. The hand correction of the semi-automatic prediction of these mappings is underway.

2.4.1   HIERARCHY OF THEMATIC ROLES

One of the immediate benefits from such a mapping is the ability to automatically cluster together PropBank argument descriptions, VerbNet semantic roles and FrameNet Frame Elements under specific PropBank argument labels. This will provide a hierarchical organization of all Agent-like (or Patient-like, or Goal-like, etc.) VerbNet roles and FrameNet Elements and allow investigations into the degrees of syntactic conformity at different levels in the hierarchy.

Note that much of this information is already implicit in the FrameNet database since many FrameNet FEs are linked via FE-FE relations to FEs in higher frames; all of the FEs descended from the Agent FE in the Transitive-action frame will be Agents of one type or another. For example, the Extradition frame inherits from Transitive-action, and the FE Authorities in Extradition inherits from the FE Agent in Transitive-action.

2.5   SUMMARY

This chapter continued the discussion of semantic role labels as essential components of the meaning representation of a sentence. It provided a brief survey of available resources that present descriptions of sets of semantic role labels for individual verb senses, along with a discussion of their linguistic motivation. These resources offer a foundation for the development of large amounts of annotated corpora which can serve as training data for supervised machine learning techniques. The next chapters focus on the task of training these machine learning systems to automatically perform semantic role labeling both for English and for other languages.

EXERCISES

1. Using the annotated Semlink corpus available at verbs.colorado.edu, examine the differences in granularity between PropBank, VerbNet and FrameNet. For a particular set of documents or verbs, how many PropBank role types are there, how many for VerbNet, how many for FrameNet? How many instances on average for each role type? What is the distribution for each lexical resource?

2. Pick 5 sentences from one of the Chapter 1 Exercise paragraphs, and assign PropBank, VerbNet and FrameNet role labels. How much information is added by the more fine-grained labels?

3. The VerbNet clear class has only 4 members. Which Frame(s) in FrameNet have the best correspondence to the verbs in this class? Why?

4. What would be appropriate selectional restrictions on these verb arguments? How could they be chosen empirically?

CHAPTER 3

Machine Learning for Semantic Role Labeling

Semantic role labeling (SRL) can be treated in the general framework of a classification task: for a given verb, and given each constituent in a parse, the task is to select from a pre-defined set the constituent's semantic role label with respect to the verb. Thus, the most basic design for a SRL system is to extract features for each constituent in a parse, and train a standard machine learning classifier (such as a maximum entropy classifier or support vector machine) to predict the label given the features. In order to evaluate our system, we can measure how many constituents are given the correct argument label.

In the following section, we will discuss features which have been used in predicting roles of individual constituents. These features are designed to capture the aspects of syntax and lexical semantics relevant to the alternation phenomena, discussed in the previous chapters, that can make semantic role labeling difficult. In order to find the best analysis of an entire sentence, we will want to extend beyond the basic design of a single decision per constituent, making decisions for constituents interdependent within a sentence, as we discuss in Section 3.4.

Our basic design also assumes a syntactic parse as an input: what is the impact of the choice of parser, its accuracy, and the choice of syntactic representation? In Section 3.5, we examine these issues, including the trade-offs between dependency- and constituent-based representations. We will also consider systems that combine parsing and semantic role labeling in order to allow semantic features to help improve the parse. In Section 3.6, we discuss methods for evaluating systems that are more forgiving in cases of parser error or mismatch between syntactic representations than the exact evaluation described above.

Our basic design also assumes training data in the form of an annotated corpus. We discuss the impact of moving to test data with different characteristics from the training data in Section 3.7. Two major resources are currently available for training: Propbank and FrameNet. In section 3.8, we discuss how the design choices of these corpora impact automatic role labeling systems and examine attempts to combine information from multiple resources.

3.1 IDENTIFICATION AND CLASSIFICATION

When syntactic parse trees are presented as input to a semantic role labeling system, one issue that immediately pops up is the large number of constituents in a parse tree due to the recursive nature of the constituents. Only a small fraction of constituents are actually arguments to some predicate in the tree. In addition, since it is not uncommon for a constituent to be assigned multiple semantic roles by different predicates (generally a predicate can only assign one semantic role to a constituent), the semantic role labeling system can only look at one predicate at a time, trying to find all the arguments for this particular predicate in the tree. The tree will be traversed as many times as there are predicates in the tree. This means there is an even higher proportion of constituents in the parse tree that are not arguments for the predicate the semantic role labeling system is currently looking at any given point. There is thus a serious imbalance between *positive samples* (constituents that are arguments to a particular predicate) and *negative samples* (constituents that are not arguments to this particular predicate). Machine learning algorithms generally do not handle extremely unbalanced data very well.

For these reasons, many systems divide the semantic role labeling task into two steps, *identification*, in which a binary decision is made as to whether a constituent carries a semantic role for a given predicate, and *classification* in which the specific semantic role is chosen. Separate machine learning classifiers are trained for these two tasks, often with many of the same features (Gildea and Jurafsky, 2002; Pradhan et al., 2005).

Another approach is to use a set of heuristics to prune out the majority of the negative samples, as a predicate's roles are generally found in a limited number of syntactic relations to the predicate itself. Some semantic labeling systems use a combination of both approaches: heuristics are first applied to prune out the constituents that are obviously not an argument for a certain predicate, and then a binary classifier is trained to further separate the positive samples from the negative samples. The goal of this filtering process is just to decide whether a constituent is an argument or not. Then a multi-class classifier is trained to decide the specific semantic role for this argument. In the filtering stage, it is generally a good idea to be conservative and err on the side of keeping too many constituents rather than being too aggressive and filtering out true arguments. This can be achieved by lowering the threshold for positive samples, or conversely, raising the threshold for negative samples.

(20)

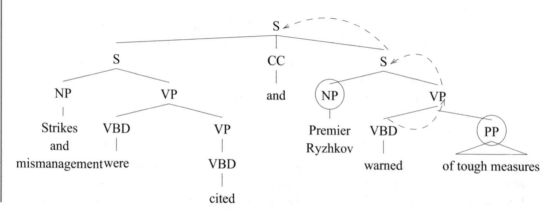

A heuristic algorithm that has been widely adopted is the one first proposed in Xue and Palmer (2004). The algorithm starts by locating the predicate for which the semantic role labeling system is identifying arguments, and then adds its sisters in the tree to the list of candidates that are potential arguments for this predicate. It then iteratively goes up a level and adds the sisters to its parent, grandparent, and so forth to the list of candidates until it reaches the root node of the tree. At each level, it first tries to decide whether there is a coordination structure. Conjuncts in a coordination structure are not possible arguments and are thus excluded from the list of candidates.

This process is illustrated in (20). Assuming that the predicate of interest is "warned," the system first adds the PP "of tough measures" to the list of candidates. It then moves up a level and adds the NP "Premier Ryzhkov" to the list of candidates. At the next level, the two S's form a coordination structure, and thus no candidate is added.

The pruning algorithm is more accurate when the parse trees that are the input to the semantic role labeling system are correct. In a realistic scenario, the parse trees are generated by a syntactic parser and are not expected to be perfect. However, experimental results show that even when the parses are imperfect, using a pruning algorithm leads to an improvement in the overall semantic role labeling accuracy.

3.2   FEATURES USED FOR CLASSIFICATION

The set of features used in SRL systems has grown over time as researchers have explored new ways of leveraging the syntactic analysis of the entire sentence to better analyze specific semantic roles. Thus, while early systems used only a handful of features, current state of the art systems use dozens. Nonetheless, the features used in the earliest systems continue to form the core of current SRL systems, and we begin by describing these core features as applied to FrameNet data by Gildea and Jurafsky (2002).

3.2.1   PHRASE TYPE

Different roles tend to be realized by different syntactic categories. For example, in FrameNet communication frames, the *Speaker* is likely to appear as a noun phrase, *Topic* as a prepositional phrase or noun phrase, and *Medium* as a prepositional phrase, as in: "[Speaker We] talked [Topic about the proposal] [Medium over the phone] ."

The phrase type feature indicates the syntactic category of the phrase expressing the semantic roles, using the set of syntactic categories of the Penn Treebank project, as described in Marcus et al. (1993). In the FrameNet data, frame elements are most commonly expressed as noun phrases (NP, 47% of frame elements in the training set), and prepositional phrases (PP, 22%). The next most common categories are adverbial phrases (ADVP, 4%), particles (e.g., "make something *up*" — PRT, 2%) and clauses (SBAR, 2%, and S, 2%).

Gildea and Jurafsky (2002) used the parser of Collins (1997), a statistical parser trained on examples from the Penn Treebank, to generate parses of the same format for the sentences in the data. Phrase types were derived automatically from parse trees generated by the parser, as shown in

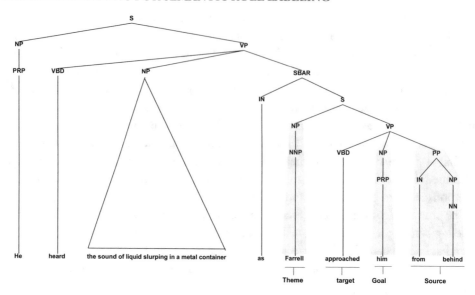

Figure 3.1: A sample sentence with parser output (above) and FrameNet annotation (below). Parse constituents corresponding to frame elements are highlighted.

Figure 3.1. Given the automatically generated parse tree, the constituent spanning the same set of words as each annotated frame element was found, and the constituent's nonterminal label was taken as the phrase type. In cases where more than one constituent matches due to a unary production in the parse tree, such as the NNP (proper noun) within the NP (noun phrase) over *Farrell* in Figure 3.1, the higher constituent was chosen.

The matching was performed by calculating the starting and ending word positions for each constituent in the parse tree, as well as for each annotated frame element, and matching each frame element with the parse constituent with the same beginning and ending points. Punctuation was ignored in this computation. Due to parsing errors, or, less frequently, mismatches between the parse tree formalism and the FrameNet annotation standards, there was sometimes no parse constituent matching an annotated frame element. In the FrameNet data, this occurred for 13% of the labels. The one case of systematic mismatch between the parse tree formalism and the FrameNet annotation standards is the FrameNet convention of including both a relative pronoun and its antecedent in frame elements, as in the first frame element in the following sentence:

(21) a. In its rough state he showed it to [$_{Agt}$ the Professor, who] **bent** [$_{BPrt}$ his grey beard] [$_{Path}$ over the neat script] and read for some time in silence.

Mismatch caused by the treatment of relative pronouns accounts for 1% of the roles in the FrameNet data.

During testing, the largest constituent beginning at the frame element's left boundary and lying entirely within the element was used to calculate the features. Gildea and Jurafsky (2002) did not use this technique on the training set, as it was expected to add noise to the data, but instead discarded examples with no matching parse constituent. The technique for finding a near match handles common parse errors such as a prepositional phrase being incorrectly attached to a noun phrase at the right-hand edge, and it guarantees that some syntactic category will be returned: the part-of-speech tag of the frame element's first word in the limiting case.

3.2.2   GOVERNING CATEGORY

The correlation between semantic roles and syntactic realization as subject or direct object is one of the primary facts that theories of Chapter 1 attempt to explain. As a basic example of how syntactic function is useful as a feature, in the sentence *He drove the car over the cliff*, the subject NP is more likely to fill the *Agent* role than the other two NPs. While some parsers produce trees annotated with such grammatical functions (Section 3.5.2), here we discuss grammatical function features that apply to syntactic trees in the standard Penn Treebank representation produced by parsers such as those of Collins (1997) and Charniak and Johnson (2005).

The first such feature, which we call "governing category," or *gov*, has only two values, S and VP, corresponding to subjects and objects of verbs, respectively. This feature is restricted to apply only to NPs as it was found to have little effect on other phrase types. As with phrase type, the feature was read from parse trees returned by the parser. We follow links from child to parent up the parse tree from the constituent corresponding to a frame element until either an S or VP node is found, and we assign the value of the feature according to whether this node is an S or VP. NP nodes found under S nodes are generally grammatical subjects, and NP nodes under VP nodes are generally objects. In most cases, the S or VP node determining the value of this feature immediately dominates the NP node, but attachment errors by the parser or constructions such as conjunction of two NPs can cause intermediate nodes to be introduced. Searching for higher ancestor nodes makes the feature robust to such cases. Even given good parses, this feature is not perfect in discriminating grammatical functions, and, in particular, it confuses direct objects with adjunct NP such as temporal phrases. For example, *town* in the sentence *He left town* and *yesterday* in the sentence *He left yesterday* will both be assigned a governing category of VP. Direct and indirect objects both appear directly under the VP node. For example, in the sentence *He gave me a new hose*, *me* and *a new hose* are both assigned a governing category of VP.

3.2.3   PARSE TREE PATH

Like the governing category feature described above, this feature is designed to capture the syntactic relation of a constituent to the rest of the sentence. However, the path feature describes the syntactic relation between the target word (that is, the predicate invoking the semantic frame) and the constituent in question, whereas the previous feature is independent of where the target word appears in the sentence; that is, it identifies all subjects whether they are the subject of the target word or not.

This feature is defined as the **path** from the target word through the parse tree to the constituent in question, represented as a string of parse tree nonterminals linked by symbols indicating upward or downward movement through the tree, as shown in Figure 3.2. Although the path is composed of a string of symbols, the system will treat the string as an atomic value. The path includes, as the first element of the string, the part of speech of the target word, and, as the last element, the phrase type or syntactic category of the sentence constituent marked as a frame element. After some experimentation, Gildea and Jurafsky (2002) used a version of the path feature that collapses the various part-of-speech tags for verbs, including past tense verb (VBD), third person singular present verb (VBZ), other present tense verb (VBP), and past participle (VBN), into a single verb tag denoted "VB."

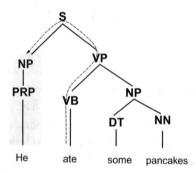

Figure 3.2: In this example, the **path** from the target word *ate* to the frame element *He* can be represented as VB↑VP↑S↓NP, with ↑ indicating upward movement in the parse tree and ↓ downward movement. The NP corresponding to *He* is found as described in Section 3.2.1.

The path feature is dependent on the syntactic representation used, which for most systems is the Treebank-2 annotation style (Marcus et al., 1994). Figure 3.3 shows the annotation for the sentence *They expect him to cut costs throughout the organization*, which exhibits the syntactic phenomenon known as subject-to-object raising, in which the main verb's object is interpreted as the embedded verb's subject. The Treebank-2 style tends to be generous in its usage of S nodes to indicate clauses, a decision intended to make possible a relatively straightforward mapping from S nodes to predications. In this example, the path from *cut* to the frame element *him* would be VB↑VP↑VP↑S↓NP, which typically indicates a verb's subject, despite the accusative case of the pronoun *him*. For the target word of *expect* in the sentence of Figure 3.3, the path to *him* would be VB↑VP↓S↓NP, rather than the typical direct object path of VB↑VP↓NP.

An example of Treebank-2 annotation of an "equi" construction, in which a noun phrase serves as an argument of both the main and subordinate verbs, is shown in Figure 3.4. Here, an empty category is used in the subject position of the subordinate clause, and is co-indexed with

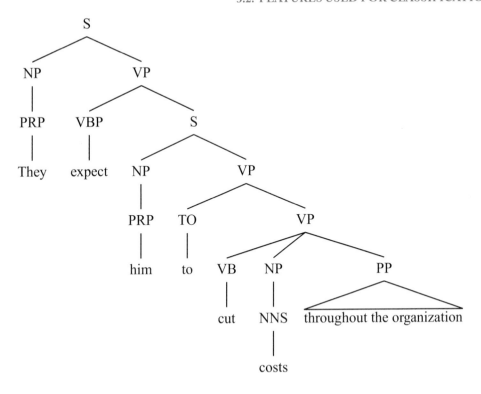

Figure 3.3: Treebank annotation of raising constructions.

the NP *Congress* in the direct object position of the main clause. The empty category, however, is not used in the statistical model of the parser or shown in its output. It is also not used by the FrameNet annotation, which would mark the NP *Congress* as a frame element of *raise* in this example. PropBank would mark both the empty category and the linked NP *Congress* with the role label. If we do not have the empty category, the value of the path feature from the target word *raise* to the frame element *Congress* would be VB↑VP↑VP↑S↑VP↓NP, and from the target word of *persuaded*, the path to *Congress* would be the standard direct object path VB↑VP↓NP.

The Treebank includes empty constituents for traces in various constructions, co-indexing relations between nodes, and secondary functional tags such as *subject* and *temporal*, all of which can help with interpretation of predicate-argument structure. However, most parser output does not include this additional information, but rather simply gives trees of phrase type categories. (For work on recovering this information automatically see Johnson (2002) and Dienes and Dubey (2003); some recent parsers have also included this information in their output (Gabbard et al., 2006).) The sentence of Figure 3.3 is one example of how the change in annotation style of Treebank-2 can affect this level of representation; the earlier style assigned the word *him* an NP node directly under the VP of *expect*.

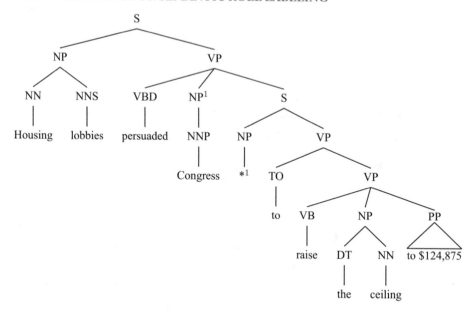

Figure 3.4: Treebank annotation of equi constructions. An empty category is indicated by *, and co-indexing by superscript [1].

The most common values of the path feature, along with interpretations, are shown in Table 3.1.

Frequency	Path	Description
	Table 3.1: Most frequent values of *path* feature in the training data.	
14.2%	VB↑VP↓PP	PP argument/adjunct
11.8	VB↑VP↑S↓NP	subject
10.1	VB↑VP↓NP	object
7.9	VB↑VP↑VP↑S↓NP	subject (embedded VP)
4.1	VB↑VP↓ADVP	adverbial adjunct
3.0	NN↑NP↑NP↓PP	prepositional complement of noun
1.7	VB↑VP↓PRT	adverbial particle
1.6	VB↑VP↑VP↑VP↑S↓NP	subject (embedded VP)
14.2		no matching parse constituent
31.4	Other	

For the purposes of choosing a frame element label for a constituent, the path feature is similar to the governing category feature defined above. Because the path captures more information, it may be more susceptible to parser errors and data sparseness. As an indication of this, the path feature takes on a total of 2,978 possible values in the training data when not counting frame elements with no matching parse constituent, and 4,086 when finding paths to the best-matching constituent in these cases. The governing category feature, on the other hand, which is defined only for NPs, has only two values (S, corresponding to subjects, and VP, corresponding to objects). In cases in which the path feature includes an S or VP ancestor of an NP node as part of the path to the target word, the governing category feature is a function of the path feature. This is the case most of the time, including for the prototypical subject (VB↑VP↑S↓NP) and object (VB↑VP↓NP) paths. Of the 35,138 frame elements identified as NPs by the parser, only 4% have a path feature that does not include a VP or S ancestor. One such example is shown in Figure 3.5, where the small clause *the remainder renting...* has no S node, giving a path feature from *renting* to *the remainder* of VB↑VP↑NP↓NP. The value of the governing category feature here is VP, as the algorithm finds the VP of the sentence's main clause as it follows parent links up the tree, spuriously in this case, as the main VP is not headed by, or relevant to, the target word *renting*.

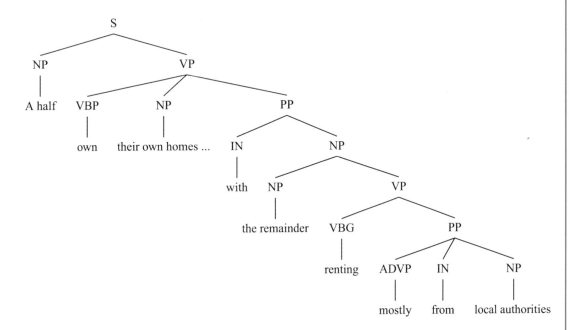

Figure 3.5: Example of target word *renting* in a small clause.

3.2.4   POSITION

In order to overcome errors due to incorrect parses, as well as to see how much can be done without parse trees, Gildea and Jurafsky (2002) use position as a feature. This feature simply indicates whether the constituent to be labeled occurs before or after the predicate defining the semantic frame. This feature is highly correlated with grammatical function, since subjects will generally appear before a verb, and objects after.

Although we do not have hand-checked parses against which to measure the performance of the automatic parser on the FrameNet corpus, the result that 13% of frame elements have no matching parse constituent gives a rough idea of the parser's accuracy. Almost all of these cases are due to parser error. Other parser errors include cases in which a constituent is found, but with the incorrect label or internal structure. This measure also considers only the individual constituent representing the frame element — the parse for the rest of the sentence may be incorrect, resulting in an incorrect value for the grammatical function features described in the previous two sections. Collins (1997) reports 88% labeled precision and recall on individual parse constituents on data from the Penn Treebank, roughly consistent with the finding of at least 13% error.

3.2.5   VOICE

The distinction between active and passive verbs plays an important role in the connection between semantic role and grammatical function, since direct objects of active verbs often correspond in semantic role to subjects of passive verbs. From the parser output, verbs were classified as active or passive by building a set of 10 passive-identifying patterns. Each of the patterns requires both a passive auxiliary (some form of *to be* or *to get*) and a past participle. Roughly 5% of the FrameNet examples were identified as passive uses; Roland (2001) reports that 6.7% of verbs are passive in the Penn Treebank Wall Street Journal corpus, and 7.8% in the Brown corpus.

3.2.6   HEAD WORD

As previously noted, lexical dependencies are extremely important in labeling semantic roles as indicated by their importance in related tasks such as parsing. Head words of noun phrases can be used to express selectional restrictions on the semantic types of role fillers. For example, in a communication frame, noun phrases headed by *Bill*, *brother*, or *he* are more likely to be the *Speaker*, while those headed by *proposal*, *story*, or *question* are more likely to be the *Topic*. (Most systems do not attempt to resolve pronoun references.)

Since the parser assigns each constituent a head word as an integral part of the parsing model, we can read the head words of the constituents from the parser output, using the same set of rules for identifying the head child of each constituent in the parse tree. The head word rules are listed in Collins (1999). Prepositions are considered to be the head words of prepositional phrases. The head word rules do not attempt to distinguish between cases in which the preposition expresses the semantic content of a role filler, such as PATH frame elements expressed by prepositional phrases headed by *along*, *through*, or *in*, and cases in which the preposition might be considered to be purely a case marker, as in most uses of *of*, where the semantic content of the role filler is expressed by the preposition's object. Complementizers are considered to be heads, meaning that infinitive verb phrases are always headed by *to*, and subordinate clauses such as in the sentence *I'm sure that he came* are headed by *that*.

3.2.7   SUBCATEGORIZATION

This feature refers to the set of a verb's syntactic arguments in the sentence. For example, we expect an intransitive use of *close* such as the *The door closed* to have a different mapping from syntactic to semantic roles when compared to the transitive use in *He closed the door*. The subcategorization feature of the first verb usage is { subject }, while the subcategorization for the second is { subject, object }.

3.2.8   ARGUMENT SET

The feature, called Frame Element Group in the FrameNet-based system of Gildea and Jurafsky (2002), is the set of all roles appearing for a verb in a given sentence. Since this feature depends on the roles assigned to all constituents in a sentence, it was employed in a post-processing ranking of role assignments for an entire sentence.

3.2.9   FEATURES INTRODUCED IN LATER SYSTEMS

We now turn from the features of Gildea and Jurafsky (2002) to those introduced by later systems; while we cannot describe every SRL system in the literature, we will try to list the features which have been found to be most important in SRL systems. The majority of these systems are trained and tested on the PropBank data; we discuss some of the issues related to the differences between the FrameNet and PropBank annotation schemes in Section 3.8.

Argument Order   This feature, introduced by Fleischman et al. (2003), is an integer indicating the position of a constituent in the sequence of arguments for the given verb. It is computed after an initial phase classifies constituents as arguments or non-arguments. Because the feature does not use the syntactic parse tree, it can help make a semantic role labeling system robust to parser error.

Previous Role   This feature, introduced by Fleischman et al. (2003), is simply the label assigned by the system to the previous argument (skipping non-argument constituents). Because this feature introduces a dependency among labels assigned to different constituents, it requires an HMM-style Viterbi search (Section 3.4.2) to find the best overall sequence for all labels in a sentence.

Head Word Part of Speech   This feature was found to boost performance by Surdeanu et al. (2003). Because Penn Treebank part of speech categories distinguish singular from plural nouns, and proper and common nouns, the part of speech tags of the head of an NP can refine the type of noun phrase involved.

Named entities in Constituents   The first of a number of features introduced by Pradhan et al. (2005), this feature uses the named entity recognizer of Bikel et al. (1999) to identify words as instances of the classes PERSON, ORGANIZATION, LOCATION, PERCENT, MONEY, TIME, and DATE. This feature helps handle the data sparsity caused by the unlimited sets of proper names for people, organizations, and locations in particular.

Verb Clustering   An automatic clustering of verbs is derived by clustering verbs according to the direct objects with which they appear using Expectation-Maximization over a latent variable model (Hofmann and Puzicha, 1998; Rooth et al., 1999). Because semantically similar verbs such as *eat* and *devour* will occur with the same objects, they will be assigned to the same clusters. The use of this cluster for predicting argument structure is motivated by the observation that semantically similar verbs undergo the same pattern of argument alternation (Levin, 1993), as discussed in Section 1.3.3.

Head Word of Objects of PPs   When a verb's argument is a prepositional phrase (PP), the PP's head word is the preposition. While this can often be a reliable indicator of semantic role (for example *in*, *across*, and *toward* usually indicate location), most prepositions can be used in many different ways, and the sense can be determined by the preposition's object. For example, *in February* indicates time, while *in New York* indicates location.

First/Last word/POS in Constituent   As with the previous feature, this feature provides more specific information about the argument filler than the headword alone, but does so in a more general way that is robust to parser error and applies to any type of constituent.

Constituent Order   This feature is related to the argument order feature above but is designed to be used in discriminating arguments from non-arguments. Pradhan et al. (2005) use a version of this feature where the position of each constituent is calculated relative to the predicate, which helps favor constituents close to the predicate.

Constituent Tree Distance   This feature has the same motivation as the previous feature but takes syntactic structure into account.

Constituent Context Features   These features provide information about the parent and left and right siblings of a constituent. For each of these three constituents, the phrase type, head word, and the head word's part of speech are given as features, for a total of nine features.

Temporal Cue Words   A number of words which indicate time, but which are not considered named entities by the named entity tagger, are included as binary features.

3.3   CHOICE OF MACHINE LEARNING METHOD

Given any set of features for each constituent in labeled data, we have a choice of a large number of methods to train a system to predict labels from new examples. The early work of Gildea and Jurafsky (2002) used a *backoff lattice*, in which probabilities of a label given various subsets of the features were calculated directly from counts in the training data, and the resulting probabilities were linearly interpolated. Less specific distributions, conditioned on fewer features, were used where no data were present for more specific feature combinations, in a method analogous to the backoff from higher- to lower-order models in *n*-gram language modeling (Katz, 1987).

However, the backoff lattice approach does not scale to larger numbers of features, and more recent work has used general-purpose machine learning algorithms. Fleischman et al. (2003) used a maximum entropy classifier, also known as logistic regression or simply as a log-linear classifier, and showed an improvement of 3.2% on role classification given role boundaries (from 78.5% to 81.7%) over the backoff lattice when using the same features. Furthermore, the maximum entropy classifier was able to take advantage of additional features added, increasing results by a further 3.0% on this task.

Surdeanu et al. (2003) used decision trees for semantic role labeling, while Pradhan et al. (2005) used support vector machines (SVMs). In a side-by-side comparison using the same features, Pradhan et al. (2005) report that decision trees yield an improvement over the backoff lattice of 2% on argument classification given boundary information, while SVMs yield a 10% improvement. Toutanova et al. (2005) used maximum entropy classifiers with the same set of features as Pradhan et al. (2005), and achieved results similar to those of the SVMs.

Overall, the experience in semantic role labeling confirms general findings in machine learning: discriminative approaches such as support vector machines and maximum entropy are better able to exploit large numbers of features than direct frequency-based models such as the lattice backoff or decision trees, both of which rapidly suffer from data sparsity due to partitioning the data on combinations of features. On many tasks, SVMs achieve better performance than maximum entropy, but the improvement is often small, and it comes at the cost of much greater training time.

3.3.1   FEATURE COMBINATIONS

Various feature combinations are found to be effective for semantic role labeling, and this is especially true for machine learning algorithms that do not consider feature combinations inherently. Machine learning algorithms such as Support Vector Machines are capable of considering feature combinations inherently at the cost of longer training time. However, Xue and Palmer (2004) show that comparable performance can be achieved by providing linguistically informed feature combinations for Maximum Entropy models, which take much less time to train than SVMs. The following feature combinations are found to be useful:

- Predicate-phrase type combination. This feature consists of the combination of the predicate lemma and the phase type of the constituent. For example, a possible feature combination might be "give-NP," if the constituent under consideration is an NP and the predicate is "give." This makes intuitive sense since given the predicate, the phrase type can be quite predictive of the semantic role of the constituent.

- Predicate-head word combination. This feature combines the predicate lemma with the head word of the constituent as a feature. This feature takes advantage of collocation information. The reasoning is that, independent of the predicate, the head word of a constituent is less informative about the semantic role of the constituent than when the predicate is known.

- Voice-position combination. This feature combines the voice on the verbal predicate with the position of the constituent under consideration. For example, a possible feature might be "before-passive," which attempts to capture information such as subject of a passive sentence, which likely plays a different semantic role than the subject of an active sentence.

When considering feature combinations, one should ensure that the feature combinations do not over fragment the training data and that they are more informative of the semantic role of the constituent in question. In practice, this is often an empirical question. Feature combinations that make sense linguistically do not always lead to improved performance and must be weighed against machine learning considerations such as sparse data problems.

3.4 JOINT INFERENCE

Many systems divide role labeling tasks into two stages, a first stage for role identification and classification of individual constituents (which may themselves be subdivided into separate tasks), and a second stage for finding the best overall labeling for all the constituents in the sentence. In this section, we discuss a number of approaches to this second stage, which we will call *joint inference*.

3.4.1 RERANKING

The early work of Gildea and Jurafsky (2002) produced a set of possible sequences of labels for the entire sentence by combining the most likely few labels for each constituent. The probabilities produced by the classifiers for individual constituents were combined with a probability for the (unordered) set of roles appearing in the entire sentence, conditioned on the predicate. This reranking step improves performance, but because of the use of frequency-based probabilities, the reranking suffers from the same inability to exploit larger numbers of features as the lattice backoff used for individual role classification. As an example, Gildea and Jurafsky (2002) did not find improved results by including the order of the role labels within the sentence.

A more sophisticated reranking system was presented by Toutanova et al. (2005) using Prop-Bank data. Here, the reranking was based on a maximum entropy model, which was combined with the maximum entropy models used to classify individual constituents. Features used in the sentence-level maximum entropy model include all the features from the individual constituent classifiers, the sequence of labels for the entire sentence (excluding Propbank's adjunct-like ARGM labels, and including the verb itself), and the sequence of untyped labels, which simply counts the number of arguments to the left and right of the verb. Another type of feature, called *frame features* by Toutanova et al. (2005), combines the role of one constituent with internal features of another. This allows the reranker to model argument-structure alternations determined by different subcategorizations of the verb, as shown by the following example from Toutanova et al. (2005):

[Arg0 Shaw Publishing] *offered* [Arg2 Mr. Smith] [Arg1 a reimbursement]

[Arg0 Shaw Publishing] *offered* [Arg1 a reimbursement] [Arg2 to Mr. Smith]

In this example, knowing that the verb's direct object is followed by a prepositional phrase will help classify the direct object as ARG1 rather than ARG2.

A drawback of the reranking approaches discussed here is that, since a fixed number of high scoring hypotheses are passed from the initial stage to the reranker, it is possible that the best overall assignment may not be among the reranker's options.

3.4.2   VITERBI SEARCH

By making simplifying assumptions about the dependencies between labels for individual constituents, we can guarantee that the best overall role assignment (at least according to the simplified model) is found. One way to do this is to make use of features consisting of adjacent pairs or triples of argument labels, essentially producing an *n*-gram language model over argument labels. The best sequence of argument labels for the entire sentence can be found by combining scores for individual labels and *n*-grams in an HMM-like Viterbi search. This approach is used by, among others, Fleischman et al. (2003) and Pradhan et al. (2005).

3.4.3   INTEGER LINEAR PROGRAMMING

Punyakanok et al. (2004) translate sentence-level constraints on role labels into the framework of an Integer Linear Programming (ILP) problem, which can then be solved with a general-purpose ILP algorithm. An ILP problem consists of an objective function to be maximized subject to certain constraints. As in Linear Programming, both the objective function and constraint functions must be linear in the variables over which the maximization takes place, such that a problem can be written in matrix notation as follows:

$$\max_{\mathbf{x}} \quad \mathbf{c}^T \mathbf{x}$$
$$\text{subject to} \quad A\mathbf{x} < 0$$
$$B\mathbf{x} = 0$$

In Integer Linear Programming, the variables $\mathbf{x}$ are further constrained to take only integer values. ILP problems are NP-complete in general, but methods have been developed that are capable of solving most instances quickly in practice. ILP solvers have the additional advantage that they can guarantee that the solution they have found is optimal.

To apply ILP to semantic role labeling, we create a binary variable $x_{ir} \in \{0, 1\}$ for each constituent i and each possible role label r. The weights $\mathbf{c}$ in the objective function are the scores for each possible label from a local classifier. Constraints can be introduced to ensure that each constituent has exactly one label in the final solution:

$$\forall i \quad \sum_r x_{ir} = 1$$

To ensure that each role label appears at most once in a sentence, we specify:

$$\forall r \quad \sum_i x_{ir} \leq 1$$

Similar constraints can be introduced to ensure that no role labels overlap in the words that they cover, to ensure that labels for discontinuous roles are consistent, and so on. Using this approach in a system based on shallow parsing (chunking) rather than full syntactic parses of the input, Punyakanok et al. (2004) report results competitive with the best systems under the same conditions from the CoNLL-04 shared task.

3.5   IMPACT OF PARSING

Most semantic role labeling systems use a syntactic parser such as those of Collins (1999) and Charniak and Johnson (2005) as a preprocessing step, identifying which spans in the input make up syntactic constituents, and producing information about grammatical relations among constituents. Since parsing is generally time consuming, especially for longer sentences, in relation to the classification of roles given the parse, it would be desirable in many situations to predict semantic roles without a full syntactic parse. In fact, the CoNLL-04 shared task (Carreras and Màrquez, 2004) investigated this situation, with a number of teams developing systems to predict role labels based on chunking, rather than parsing, information. The chunks essentially provide information corresponding to one level of the full parse: base noun phrases, verbs phrases, and so on. The best systems achieved an F_1 score of 70%, but were trained on less data than the other systems discussed here. In a more direct comparison Carreras and Màrquez (2005) report only a 2.18 point degradation in performance using only shallow parses rather than full parses on the same data, but it should be noted that this full-parse system is still 4.47 points below the best performers on the task. Thus, it seems that role labeling without parsing does come at a cost in accuracy, due to the need to use more complex grammatical relations, as well as the fact that roles are generally defined in PropBank with respect to complete, rather than base level, constituents. For example, when a noun phrase contains a prepositional phrase, the complete noun phrase is almost always labeled as the verb's argument, rather than just the base noun phrase excluding the PP.

3.5.1   INTEGRATED PARSING AND SRL

Although using the output of a parser improves semantic role labeling, parser error is one of the major sources of error in current systems. Using gold standard parse trees from the Penn Treebank improves a system's F_1 score by as much as ten points: for example from 79% to 91% in the experiments of Pradhan et al. (2005). A major reason is that, if a particular span of the input sentence is not recognized as a constituent by the parser, it will never be correctly classified by the labeling system. This has inspired work on integrating semantic role labeling and parsing in order to improve the underlying parser with semantic information. Gildea and Jurafsky (2002) did not find an improvement from adding probabilities from semantic role labels into the generative model of the Collins (1999) parser. Yi and Palmer (2005) added semantic role information to a maximum entropy parser based on that of Ratnaparkhi (1997) but also did not find improved SRL accuracy. Sutton and McCallum (2005) used features from semantic role labeling to rerank a list of k-best parses according to the Collins model, but, again, without finding improved SRL accuracy.

Merlo and Musillo (2008) use node labels from PropBank as features in a discriminatively trained parser that builds trees containing role labels but lacking the bindings between argument roles and the governing predicate. A separate post-processing classifier makes these binding decisions using SVMs. While this technique does not show improvement on the evaluation of syntactic trees according to standard parsing metrics, performance on the semantic role labeling task is competitive with the top systems.

Another approach to integrating the semantic role labels of PropBank with syntactic parsing is use of PropBank to enrich and re-analyze the annotation of the Penn Treebank. Shen et al. (2008) use PropBank annotation to guide an automatic conversion of the Treebank to a Lexicalized Tree Adjoining Grammar (LTAG) representation. Tree Adjoining Grammar (Joshi et al., 1975; Abeillé and Rambow, 2001) takes tree fragments as elementary units analogous to nonterminals of a context-free grammar and allows them to combine with the operations of substitution and adjunction. In the LTAG-spinal representation of Shen et al. (2008), the elementary trees of the grammar are subtrees of the parse tree from the Penn Treebank, consisting of one word from the original sentence and a chain of its direct ancestors in the tree. Other elementary trees that attach to a word's tree fragment can be thought of as arguments or modifiers of the word. Thus, the PropBank annotation can be used to help select among decompositions of the original parse tree. Shen and Joshi (2008) develop a statistical parser for this LTAG representation and measure its performance in terms of the number of word-to-word dependencies correctly recovered. Performance is comparable to dependency-level evaluation of other state-of-the-art parsers, though this does not measure whether the dependencies of the LTAG-spinal Treebank are in fact closer to the true semantics of the sentences. The parser is not evaluated in terms of recovery of PropBank argument labels, however.

3.5.2   CHOICE OF SYNTACTIC REPRESENTATION

Combinatory Categorial Grammar (CCG) (Steedman, 2000) defines types for predicates in terms of the arguments they expect. The essential operation in the construction of a valid syntactic tree in this framework is the combination of a predicate with one of its required arguments, which would seem to be a natural fit for semantic role labeling. Since the type representations of predicates in

CCG are somewhat abstracted from the particular syntactic structures they appear in, the CCG representation will more naturally capture long-distance dependencies (e.g., relative clauses) than a context-free phrase structure grammar would. This reduces the complexity that the semantic role labeler itself must model. An SRL system taking the output of CCG parser was trained and tested by Gildea and Hockenmaier (2003), who found improved performance on core arguments in Propbank. The CCG parser was that of Hockenmaier and Steedman (2002), which was trained on an automatic conversion of the Penn Treebank to the CCG syntactic representations.

Lexical Tree Adjoining Grammar (LTAG), as mentioned in the previous section, also provides a natural match to SRL for similar reasons as CCG: in the LTAG representation, the core, required arguments of a predicate correspond to substitution sites in the predicate's elementary tree, and optional adjuncts (ARGM in PropBank terminology) correspond to trees adjoined into a predicate's elementary tree. An SRL system based on this LTAG representation was presented by Chen and Rambow (2003), who found improved performance on core arguments.

Dependency-based representations model the syntax of a sentence as a set of binary relations between words, which form a directed tree. The dependency tree has exactly as many nodes as there are words in the sentence, unlike constituent trees for which, while the leaves of the tree correspond to the words of the sentence, different numbers of internal nodes may be proposed in different theories of syntax or syntactic annotation schemes. While dependency representations are often extracted from the output of constituent-based parsers using a set of deterministic head rules, dependency-based parsers such as those of McDonald et al. (2005) and Nivre et al. (2006), which generate such representations directly from text, have gained popularity in recent years. A major reason is the ability of dependency parsers to generate *non-projective* trees, in which a word and its dependents may span a discontinuous portion of the sentence. Non-projective trees are more common in languages such as Czech than in English, but they can be used to represent discontinuous PropBank arguments even in English for sentences such as:

[$_{Arg1}$ Million dollar conferences] were [$_{Pred}$ held] to [$_{Arg1}$ chew on such subjects as ...] or, the most common type of discontinuous argument:

[$_{Arg1}$ The agreement,] [$_{Arg0}$ Mary] [$_{Pred}$ said,] [$_{Arg1}$ was never intended to be permanent]

The CoNLL 2008 shared task (Surdeanu et al., 2008) focused on SRL in this type of representation and compared a large number of such systems. Among the best such systems, Johansson and Nugues (2008) showed that dependency-based SRL can perform comparably to state-of-the-art constituent-based systems, and can outperform on dependency-based evaluation measures (Section 3.6).

3.5.3   COMBINING PARSERS

Since different parsers make different mistakes, there may be some benefit to allowing an SRL system to choose among the output of several parsers, even if choosing among one parser's k-best list does not prove beneficial. This approach was explored by Pradhan et al. (2005). In this work, features from a statistical parser based on Combinatory Categorial Grammar (CCG) were added to an SVM-based system based on the Penn Treebank parser of Charniak (2000). Results are combined with SRL systems trained on two very different representations: the output of the Minipar parser (Lin, 1998) and the output of a nonrecursive syntactic chunking system. Among these parsers, the CCG parser differs from the Penn Treebank representation produced by the Collins or Charniak parsers, but still ultimately derives from statistics computed over the same training data. Minipar is not statistical, and hence not based on the Treebank data, and furthermore represents many grammatical constructions quite differently than the Treebank. Pradhan et al. (2005) showed an improvement of 0.5 F_1 score from adding CCG features. In order to allow for the differences between representations, Pradhan et al. (2005) adopted headword-based scoring, under which the semantic roles labels for both system output and the gold standard are assigned to the constituents' headwords, and the system output is considered correct if it assigns a role to the correct headword, without necessarily finding the correct beginning and end point of the argument. Under this scoring metric, combining the system based on the Charniak parser with Minipar improved results by 0.8 points, and combining these two with the chunk-based system yielded a further 0.7 points.

3.6 EVALUATION

The basic evaluation measure mentioned at the beginning of this chapter is to measure the number of arguments for which a system has found the correct beginning and end points, and the correct label. A common approach is to do this separately for each predicate, providing the positions of the predicates to be analyzed as input to the system. Systems may differ in the overall number of arguments that they identify, leading to a trade-off between precision (the percentage of the labels output by the system which are correct) and recall (the percentage of the true labels correctly identified by the system). A common method for combining precision and recall into a single number in order to compare systems is F-measure, which is the harmonic mean of precision and recall:

$$F = \frac{2PR}{P + R}$$

A more general measure, F_β, provides a weighted combination for a specified value of β:

$$F_\beta = \frac{(1 + \beta^2)PR}{\beta^2 P + R}$$

The standard F-measure corresponds to choosing a default value of 1 for β.

A number of evaluations have relaxed the assumption that the boundaries of the argument must match the gold standard exactly. A common approach is to identify the head word of the argument in both the gold standard and system output and give the system credit whenever the head words match, regardless of the boundaries of the rest of the argument. This allows systems to be penalized less harshly when parser error makes it impossible to identify the exact boundaries, and it can also make evaluation less sensitive to differences in the syntactic representation used, for example the difference between the Penn Treebank and derived CCG representations discussed in Section 3.5.2.

Finally, while early SRL systems were given the predicate of interest as input, a complete language understanding system must also find and disambiguate the predicates themselves. Thus, some system evaluations require the system to identify predicates and, in some cases, choose among the senses as defined by the dataset: rolesets in the case of PropBank or frames in the case of FrameNet. In this setting, it is common to score accuracy over predicate-argument relations, where both the predicate and argument must be correct for the relation to be scored as correct.

It can also be instructive to examine the number of predicates for which all arguments are correct, which we refer to as proposition-level scoring. This naturally results in a much smaller number than measuring argument-level accuracy; for example, a system with an argument-level F-measure of .80 may only achieve a proposition-level F-measure of .54 (Surdeanu et al., 2008).

3.7   GENRE

Because statistical natural language processing systems rely heavily on data specific to individual words, they are often sensitive to discrepancies between the genre or topic of the training and test data. While the Penn Treebank Wall Street Journal (WSJ) data is the largest corpus annotated with syntactic parses, it represents a fairly narrow range of style and topic: heavily edited newspaper text, predominantly financial. Semantic role labeling systems are not immune to domain adaptation problems, and may be especially vulnerable given that each predicate can behave differently, and PropBank role labels are defined relative to individual verbs.

The Penn Treebank does include parse trees for a portion of the Brown corpus of Kučera and Francis (1967), which contains text from a variety of genres. PropBank contains semantic role labels for this data, allowing us to compare the performance of systems trained on one genre and tested on another. The CoNLL-04 shared task examined this condition, with all teams submitting results trained on the WSJ and tested on both WSJ and Brown. Performance drops significantly on Brown for all participants, by anywhere from 8 points to 12 for the best performing systems.

3.8   CHOICE OF RESOURCES AND COMBINATION OF RESOURCES

Most semantic role labeling systems are based on PropBank, but it is interesting to consider how the decisions involved in constructing such a resource effect the end results. FrameNet's frames tend to have a larger number of labels (frame elements) appearing with a given verb than PropBank, making the task generally more difficult (Litkowski, 2004; Kwon et al., 2004), despite the fact that FrameNet's frame elements capture generalizations across predicates appearing in the same frame.

One recent line of work attempts to improve SRL by exploiting connections between Prop-Bank, FrameNet, VerbNet, and related resources (Shi and Mihalcea, 2005; Giuglea and Moschitti,

2006; Yi et al., 2007; Merlo and van der Plas, 2009). While PropBank's role labels are defined relative to each predicate, most systems use some features that are verb-specific and others that are not, meaning that system designers have found it beneficial to take advantage of the fact that there is in fact some consistency in what a given argument number means for different verbs. This issue is examined more closely by Yi et al. (2007), who label arguments from the PropBank data with a set of roles from VerbNet (see Section 2.2), which defines thematic roles such as AGENT, PATIENT, and TOPIC for a large number of English verbs in each of their alternation patterns (Kipper et al., 2000; Kipper Schuler, 2005). Using this level of representation is found to improve SRL results, in particular for PropBank's *Arg2*, which varies widely in interpretation across verbs. This method also helps address the genre-dependency discussed above: thematic role labels increase performance in identifying *Arg2* by 6 points for WSJ test data, but 10 points for Brown test data. Efforts to link the PropBank and FrameNet resources to one another, and to define semantics for the roles used by each resource, such as the efforts discussed in Section 2.4, are a likely avenue for future improvements in semantic role labeling systems.

Another study showing the benefit of VerbNet's Intersective Levin Classes (ILC) for semantic role labeling was that of Giuglea and Moschitti (2006), who automatically mapped FrameNet frames to ILCs, and then trained an automatic classifier to identify the ILC of new words in text. These automatically generated ILC labels proved to be a good substitute for the FrameNet frame in a complete semantic role labeling system, allowing one to better generalize to verbs not yet covered by the FrameNet project's data.

3.9   UNSUPERVISED AND PARTIALLY SUPERVISED APPROACHES

Fürstenau and Lapata (2009) take a partially supervised approach to increase the amount of training data for individual predicates by first finding unlabeled sentences that are similar to labeled sentences according to syntactic and semantic features, and then projecting the argument labels from the labeled to the unlabeled sentence. For each labeled sentence in the training data, only the most similar unlabeled examples are chosen, limited to a fixed number of new examples derived from each labeled sentence – the best results were found with 2 new examples. By restricting the label projection to these high-confidence examples, a significant improvement is achieved over using the labeled data alone.

Another use for partially supervised approaches comes from the need to generalize to predicates for which no labeled data are available. Gordon and Swanson (2007) generalize to new predicates by projecting argument labels to new predicates from syntactically similar predicates from the labeled training data. Syntactic similarity is measured in terms of the frequencies with which verbs appear with various syntactic arguments, determined by the parse tree path. Words for which the vectors of counts of argument types are similar (according to a cosine measure) are considered syntactically similar. Gordon and Swanson (2007) find a drop in precision of about 10% in moving from predicates for which training data are available to new predicates, based on a simple semantic role labeling systems that uses parse tree path as the only feature.

Another unsupervised approach to semantic role labeling is taken by Swier and Stevenson (2004), who use VerbNet to constrain possible thematic roles for arguments of verbs, and then bootstrap a classifier which successively adds training data for which it can make confident predictions. This approach can only be applied to verbs for which a dictionary of syntactic-semantic argument linking such as VerbNet has been produced; a more general unsupervised method is attempted by Grenager and Manning (2006), who learn linkings of a set of syntactic positions to semantic roles by applying expectation maximization (EM). The EM algorithm learns the parameters of a probability model where the choice of linking is conditioned on the verbs, and the head word of the argument is conditioned on the semantic role. To reduce the space of possible linkings, linkings can only be constructed by applying a set of pre-specified operations such as "make the subject ARG0." The set of operations provides the model with some general information about English grammar, but the model is trained without using any annotated semantic roles. Despite this, Grenager and Manning (2006) show that their system can do better at assigning Propbank labels to new data than a simple baseline which always assigns the most frequent argument label to each syntactic position.

EXERCISES

1. Using the Penn Treebank parse trees and the argument labels from the PropBank distribution, write feature extraction routines to compute, for each argument, the values of the phrase type, governing category, parse tree path, position, voice, head word, subcategorization, and argument set features described in this chapter.

2. How informative is each feature as to the PropBank argument type? Compute the conditional entropy of the argument type given the feature to try to estimate this. How accurate is a labeling system based on simply selecting the argument label with the highest probability given each feature?

3. Using a general-purpose maximum entropy machine learning toolkit, train a system to predict argument label given the set of features extracted in the previous exercise. Experiment with various subsets of features and values of the prior on feature weights to optimize performance on a held-out test set.

CHAPTER 4

A Cross-Lingual Perspective

In this chapter, we discuss semantic role labeling from a multilingual perspective. We start with a brief description of the different styles of semantic role annotation carried out across languages. We then present the problem of semantic role projection, the task of automatically transferring semantic roles from one language to another. Semantic role projection is a way of tackling the semantic role labeling problem when no manual annotation is available for a particular language. The second topic we discuss in this chapter is semantic role alignment, which addresses the issue of aligning predicate-argument structures in parallel data. The prerequisite for this task is that semantic role annotation exists in both languages of the parallel data. The third and final topic of the chapter is semantic role adaptation. We discuss the similarities and differences in semantic role labeling from a cross-linguistic perspective. Our discussion is focused on Chinese, where there exist multiple fully developed systems. We show that while the general formulation of semantic role labeling as a machine learning problem works well in Chinese, as in English, a semantic role labeling system must incorporate language-specific properties to reach its full potential.

Since Semantic Role Labeling (SRL) was first introduced, the task has attracted great interest, showing a trend in statistical natural language processing of moving from syntactic parsing to deeper semantic analysis. The popularity of SRL is spreading to languages other than English where the necessary linguistic resources are being built or have already been built and systems for automatic semantic role labeling are starting to emerge. For example, significant amount of semantically annotated resources already exist for Chinese (Xue and Palmer, 2009), Czech (Böhmová et al., 2003), Japanese (Lida et al., 2007; Ohara, 2008), German (Burchardt et al., 2006), Catalan and Spanish (Taulé et al., 2008). Pilot annotation has also been performed for Arabic (Palmer et al., 2008) and Korean (Palmer et al., 2006). Semantic role labeling systems are starting to be developed using these linguistic resources (Xue, 2008; Surdeanu et al., 2008; Diab et al., 2008).

At a very basic level, supervised machine-learning systems work by learning from human annotated data. As a result, the output of a machine-learning based semantic role labeling system is to a large extent determined by the annotated corpus. Although the semantic annotation projects mentioned above all target the predicate-argument structure and label the role the argument plays with respect to the predicate, the actual labels that are used to characterize these roles vary from project to project, as discussed in Chapter 2. They generally fall into the following three broad categories: Propbank-style roles, FrameNet-style roles, and roles that are defined based on the linguistic traditions of a particular language.

Propbank-type labels   A number of these semantically annotated resources use Propbank-style roles, and these include the Chinese Propbank (Xue and Palmer, 2009), the Korean Propbank (Palmer et al., 2006), the Pilot Arabic Propbank (Palmer et al., 2008), and AnCora (Taulé et al., 2008) for Catalan and Spanish. In fact, the Chinese, Korean, and Arabic Propbanks are developed in close association with one another by the same key researchers, and among those, the Chinese Propbank is the most substantial in size. It currently has close to one million words annotated on data that include newswire, magazine articles, broadcast news, and broadcast conversations. The AnCora corpus, developed jointly by several groups of researchers in Spain, also uses Propbank-style roles. As discussed in Chapter 2, the Propbank-style annotation is characterized by predicate-specific roles for core arguments which are assigned numerical values prefixed by "Arg-" (*Arg0* through *Arg5*), plus adjunctive roles that are predicate-independent. The roles for core arguments are predicate-specific in the sense that they can only be interpreted in the context of a specific predicate. Although there is some consistency in how *Arg0* and *Arg1* are defined, there is quite a bit of variation in the meaning of *Arg2* through *Arg5*. *Arg0* is the prototypical agent while *Arg1* is the prototypical patient. *Arg2*, on the other hand, can be beneficiary, goal, source, extent or cause. While the core arguments are more important to the predicate and the latter often imposes selectional constraints on the former, there are no such constraints on adjunctive arguments. The adjunctive arguments are thus characterized by roles such as location (*ArgM-LOC*), temporality (*ArgM-TMP*), and manner (*ArgM-MNR*). The predicate-specific nature of the Propbank-style semantic roles seems fairly intuitive to annotators. Guided by *frame files* where semantic roles are defined for each predicate, annotators are able to achieve high inter-annotator agreement, which is essential to the viability of a resource for machine learning purposes. Palmer et al. (2005) reports inter-annotator agreement of above ninety percent by Kappa metrics for the English Propbank, and this explains in part the success of this corpus as a computational linguistic resource.

FrameNet-style labels   FrameNet (Baker et al., 1998) is another widely used semantic annotation resource whose annotation framework has been adopted by semantic annotation projects for other languages. In particular, it has been adopted in the SALSA Project for German (Burchardt et al., 2006), the Japanese FrameNet Project (Ohara, 2008), and the Spanish FrameNet Project (Subirats and Petruck, 2003). As discussed in Chapter 2, FrameNet defines a very different set of semantic roles. The predicate in the FrameNet annotation framework is called *Lexical Unit (LU)* and the semantic roles are called *Frame Elements (FE)* and they are organized by *semantic frames*, which are conceptual structures that describe a particular situation or event along with its participants. FEs are defined for each semantic frame, and all LUs in a semantic frame share the same set of semantic roles. The semantic roles in FrameNet are more general than those in the PropBank in the sense that the semantic roles in the former are interpretable with respect to a semantic frame, not just to individual predicates. For example, the verbs *buy* and *sell* both belong to the semantic frame *Commerce_buy*, which involves a *Buyer* and *Seller* exchanging *Money* and *Goods*. Buyer and Goods are *core* FEs for this frame while Seller and Money are Non-Core FEs. Other

Non-Core FEs include but are not limited to *Duration*, the length of time the Goods are in the Buyer's possession, *Manner*, the manner in which the transaction is performed, *Means*, the means by which the transaction takes place, *Place*, the location where the transaction occurs, *Rate*, and *Unit*, the unit of measure for the *Goods*.

Semantic Roles of Other Flavors   Not all semantic role annotation projects follow the lead of FrameNet or Propbank. The Prague Dependency Treebank (PDT) (Böhmová et al., 2003), for example, has its own style of semantic annotation. The tectogrammatical layer of the PDT is a layer of semantic annotation that targets the predicate-argument structure. Like Propbank and FrameNet, the PDT also has a notion of core vs peripheral arguments although the boundary may not be drawn along the exact same lines as those in FrameNet and Propbank. The PDT makes a distinction between *inner participants* and *free modifications*. Inner participants are roughly core arguments while free modifications are roughly adjunctive arguments. Inner participants are "such modifications that can modify a given verb only once (except for the case of coordination) and they only modify a more or less closed class of verbs that can be listed." Free modifications, on the other hand, are "such modifications that can - if it is not excluded for semantic reasons - modify any verb (word) and they can modify a particular verb (word) more than once" (Mikulová et al., 2006) . There are five roles for inner participants, *Actor*, *Patient*, *Addressee*, *Origo*, and *Effect* for verbal predicates, and one additional role *MAT* for nominal predicates. MAT (material, partitive) represents an adnominal argument denoting the content (people, things, substance etc.) of a container expressed by the governing noun. Roles for free modifications correspond to temporal, locative/directional, manner, and other kinds of adverbials.

The Kyoto University Text Corpus[1] (Kawahara et al., 2002) and the NAIST Text Corpus (Lida et al., 2007) are strongly influenced by Japanese linguistic traditions. Although the two corpora differ in the annotation of specific linguistic constructions, both corpora take advantage of the close association between the grammatical cases and the semantic roles, and label the arguments based on their grammatical case. Arguments are labeled with nominative (GA), accusative (O) and dative (NI) cases. However, Japanese semantic role labeling is not as simple as identifying the case markers since these case markers are routinely dropped in actual Japanese text. In addition, word order is considered to be less rigid for Japanese than for languages like English and Chinese, potentially increasing the level of difficulty for Japanese semantic role labeling.

It is worth noting that while Propbank and FrameNet both assign semantic roles to constituents in a parse tree or the text spans of the constituents, the semantic roles for both Czech and Japanese are assigned to words directly, essentially treating the semantic roles as a dependency relation between the predicate and (the head of) its argument.

---

[1] http://www-lab25.kuee.kyoto-u.ac.jp/nl-resource/corpus-e.html

4.1   SEMANTIC ROLE PROJECTION

Creating a semantically annotated resource such as the Propbank or the FrameNet requires substantial time and monetary investment, and there have been efforts in recent years to circumvent this data bottleneck when conducting research in semantic role labeling. One line of research takes advantage of the availability of parallel data (Padó and Lapata, 2005; Johansson and Nugues, 2006; Fung et al., 2007) to project semantic role annotation from a resource-rich language to a resource-poor language. English is by far the language with the most linguistic resources, and it is usually the source language from which semantic role annotation is projected. For semantic role projection to work, there has to be parallel data in addition to semantic role annotation on the source language. The semantic role information on the source side of the parallel data does not have to be manually annotated, but manual annotation has to exist on source language data in sufficient amount to train an automatic semantic role labeling system. The semantic role labeling system can then be used to automatically annotate the source side of the parallel data so that the semantic roles can be projected onto the target side.

After the source side of the parallel data has been annotated with semantic role information either manually or automatically, the next step in semantic role projection is to word-align the parallel data. Word alignment tools are readily available. For example, GIZA++ (Och and Ney, 2003), a language-independent word alignment tool, is publicly available and can be retrained to word-align parallel data for any language pair. With word-aligned parallel data and semantic role annotation on the source side, there are a number of ways that the semantic role annotation can be transferred to the target side. Padó and Lapata (2005) defined word-based and constituent-based models of semantic role transfer. In a word-based model, the semantic role of a source span is assigned to all target tokens that are aligned to some token in the source span. This simple approach does not guarantee that the target tokens aligned to a source span cover a consecutive span of text, over which semantic roles are typically defined. There may be "holes" in the string of target tokens mapped from a source span. Padó and Lapata show that they are able to improve the semantic role projection accuracy by simply plugging in those holes and assigning the semantic role for a pair of non-adjacent words w_i and w_j also to the words in between if w_i and w_j have the same semantic role.

A more effective approach is a constituent-based model where the constituents rather than words are aligned. Constituent-based alignment makes intuitive sense because both Propbank and FrameNet styles of semantic roles are defined over syntactic constituents. In addition, in a constituent alignment model, not all words in a constituent have to be aligned for the constituent alignment to be correct. For example, function words in a source constituent may not occur in the target constituent and vice versa. In not requiring that all words be aligned between the source and target constituents, word alignment errors can also be remedied to some extent. For constituent-based alignment to work, the constituents have to be generated either with a full syntactic parser or a non-recursive syntactic chunker. One can imagine several different scenarios in which constituents can be aligned. The alignment can go from the source side to the target side, or vice versa. Given a constituent from the source side or the target side, the problem of constituent alignment is one of finding the most probable constituent on the other side that is aligned with it. One way to choose the most probable constituent is to define a similarity metric between the source and target constituent. Padó and Lapata show that the most effective metric is one that is defined over aligned content words. The similarity metric is defined over the overlap between word tokens in source constituent c_s and target constituent c_t. The overlap of c_s and c_t is the proportion of tokens in c_t aligned with tokens in c_s. Conversely, the overlap of c_t and c_s is the proportion of tokens in c_s that are aligned with some token in c_t. Notice that there is an asymmetry in this relationship, and the overlap for the two directions is not necessarily the same because the number of tokens in the source and target constituent is not necessarily the same. To address this, Padó and Lapata define the similarity as the product of the two overlaps, as in Equation 4.1:

$$sim(c_s, c_t) = O(c_s, c_t) \cdot O(c_t, c_s) \tag{4.1}$$

The overlap in content words between source constituent c_s and target constituent c_t is calculated with Equation 4.2, where t_s is a token in c_s, $yield(c)$ denotes the set of content tokens in the yield of a constituent c, and $al(t_s)$ denotes the tokens aligned to t_s.

$$O(c_s, c_t) = \frac{| \cup_{t_s \in yield(c_s)} al(t_s) \cap yield(c_t) |}{| yield(c_t) |} \tag{4.2}$$

The calculation of $O(c_t, c_s)$ works in the same way, and it can be computed with Equation 4.3, where t_t is a token in c_t, and $al(t_t)$ denotes the tokens aligned to t_t.

$$O(c_t, c_s) = \frac{| \cup_{t_t \in yield(c_t)} al(t_t) \cap yield(c_s) |}{| yield(c_s) |} \tag{4.3}$$

In a *forward constituent alignment* model a_f, source constituents that form the span of a semantic role are aligned to a single target constituent. The similarity of a target constituent c_t to a set of source constituents a_s for a role r can be computed by taking the product of the similarity between each source and target constituent pair, as in Equation 4.4. The c_t with the highest similarity score to $a_s(r)$ among all constituents C_t in the target sentence is chosen as the correct alignment.

$$a_f(a_s, sim, r) = \underset{c_t \in C_t}{\mathrm{argmax}} \prod_{c_s \in a_s(r)} sim(c_s, c_t) \tag{4.4}$$

An example is presented in Figure 4.1 where the similarity scores for each source and target constituent pair are shown in a table. For example, the similarity between XP_2 and YP_6 is computed as $O(XP_2, YP_6) \cdot O(YP_6, XP_2) = 1/3 \cdot 1/2 = 0.167$.

Johansson and Nugues (2006) took semantic role projection a step further in their work on Swedish semantic role labeling. Since there was no manually annotated data in Swedish, Johansson and Nugues started by training a semantic role labeler for English, and then they tagged the English side of an English-Swedish parallel corpus. The semantic roles on the English side are then projected onto the Swedish side using a procedure similar to the word-alignment based model described in

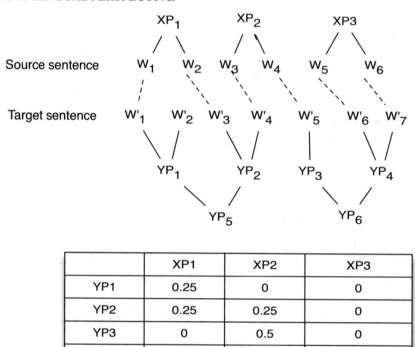

	XP1	XP2	XP3
YP1	0.25	0	0
YP2	0.25	0.25	0
YP3	0	0.5	0
YP4	0	0	1
YP5	0.5	0.125	0
YP6	0	0.167	0.667

Figure 4.1: A semantic role projection example. W_1, W_2, ... W_6 are words in the source sentence, XP_1, XP_2, XP_3 are constituents in the source sentence, W'_1, W'_2, ... W'_7 are words in the target sentence, and YP_1, YP_2, ..., YP_6 are constituents in the target sentence.

Padó and Lapata (2005). Using the Swedish side of the parallel corpus as training corpus, they then developed a Swedish semantic role labeler, using an SVM classifier. Their system achieved a precision of 0.67 and a recall of 0.47, and they observed that the accuracy of the Swedish semantic role labeler in terms of F-measure is very close to the product of the accuracy of the English semantic role labeler and the semantic role projection accuracy from English to Swedish.

The promise of semantic role projection research hinges on a few assumptions that have yet to be verified. First of all, as pointed out by Johansson and Nugues, it assumes that the semantic role annotation framework in the source language is also meaningful in the target language. It also assumes that a predicate in the source language is always translated into a predicate with the same semantic roles in the target language. Neither assumption can be taken for granted, but judging by the semantic role projection accuracy, these assumptions seem to hold at least to some extent.

There is also reason to believe that these assumptions may hold better for some language pairs than others, and for literal translation than free translation. As a result, we would expect that semantic role projection accuracy will also fluctuate along these dimensions.

4.2   SEMANTIC ROLE ALIGNMENT

As semantically annotated corpora become available in multiple languages, a question that naturally arises is how consistent the semantic annotation is across languages. While all semantic role annotation by definition targets the predicate-argument structure, different annotation projects may use different semantic role inventories. In addition, given a specific predicate, it may not always be possible to find a predicate in another language with the exact same number and type of arguments (Padó and Erk, 2005; Padó, 2007). In actual parallel data, a given predicate in the source language may be translated into multiple predicates in the target language. How well the arguments for predicates that are translations of each other are aligned in actual parallel text is an empirical question that is worth investigating. The problem can be formulated as a semantic role alignment task where the arguments for a pair of source and target predicates can be aligned, and the accuracy of such an alignment algorithm can be empirically evaluated given gold standard annotation data.

Semantic role alignment is a different problem than semantic role projection, and it assumes that semantic role annotation is already available on both sides of the parallel data, but the semantic role annotation is performed independently, and the semantic role labels for the source and target languages are not necessarily the same. For example, *Arg0* in one language might correspond to *Arg1* in another language for Propbank-style annotation, and this happens when the same role is annotated with different labels in different languages. If the semantic role annotation is the output of an automatic semantic role labeling system, there will also be errors in the textual boundaries of the argument as well as the roles assigned to the argument. It is meaningful to evaluate how well the semantic roles can be automatically aligned in view of its potential application in Machine Translation and other natural language systems. The hope is that semantic structures in the form of semantic roles can better survive translation than syntactic structures. Figure 4.2 provides an example of aligned predicate-argument structures between a Chinese and English sentence. The syntactic structure does not survive the translation: the Chinese verbal predicate 怀疑 ("doubt") is translated into an English noun "doubt," and the Chinese prepositional phrase "对 (toward) 另外 (other) 99 条 (classifier) 新闻 (news)" is translated into a English noun phrase "the other 99 pieces of news." However, the predicate-argument structure abstracts away from the syntactic structure so that, at the predicate argument structure level, the Chinese predicate is still a predicate in English, and a Chinese argument is mapped onto an English argument. For such semantic structures to benefit machine translation, the semantic role alignment must be performed with reasonable accuracy.

Fung et al. (2007) reported a first attempt to align predicate-argument structures between Chinese and English. Given a source language sentence S_s and target sentence S_t, Fung et al. proposed an algorithm that first aligns the predicates in the source and target sentence. The alignment of the predicates requires either a bilingual dictionary or a word alignment tool such as GIZA++. Then

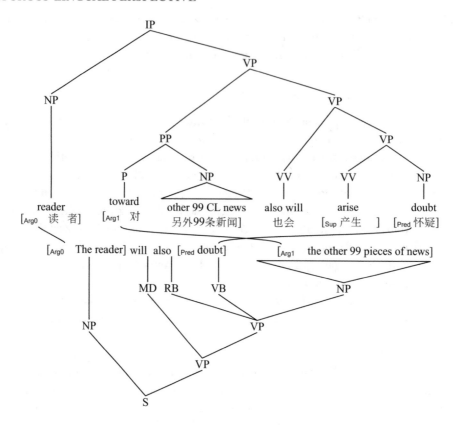

Figure 4.2: Semantic role alignment between Chinese and English

for each predicate pair *PRED_s* and *PRED_t*, their arguments are extracted. As far as the alignment algorithm is concerned, the arguments can be manually annotated or automatically produced by a semantic role labeling system. For each source argument, a similarity metric is used to determine the highest ranked target argument that is aligned to it. The calculation of the similarity metric requires that the words in the source and target arguments be word-aligned and again this can be achieved with a word alignment tool or a bilingual dictionary. Fung et al. use the cosine similarity (Equation 4.5) in their experiments to align the source and target arguments and show that the arguments are correctly aligned with an accuracy of 0.725 by F-measure. A pair of arguments are correctly aligned if the arguments are correctly labeled by the automatic semantic role labeling system, and the source argument is aligned to the correct target argument. They also show that the semantic role alignment accuracy is higher than the semantic role projection accuracy (46.63%) between Chinese and English, assuming the semantic roles are projected from English to Chinese. The results are as expected, given that a semantic role projection task does not take advantage of the manually annotated semantic data on the Chinese side.

$$sim(ARG_i, ARG_j) = \frac{ARG_i \cdot ARG_j}{|ARG_i||ARG_j|} \qquad (4.5)$$

Choi et al. (2009) also reported work that uses aligned predicate-argument structures between English and Chinese to improve word alignment. The idea is that given semantic role labeled sentences on both sides of a parallel Chinese-English corpus, if a Chinese argument is not aligned with an English argument that has the same semantic role label, it is probably due to an error in word alignment. This information can then be used to help correct the word alignment errors.

4.3   LANGUAGE-(IN)DEPENDENT SEMANTIC ROLE LABELING

In the reminder of this chapter, we discuss how semantic role labeling techniques developed for one language can be adapted for use in another language. We attempt to explore the issue of language (in)dependence of semantic role labeling techniques. Language independence is often used as a measure to determine superiority of language processing techniques, but drawing results primarily from research in Chinese semantic role labeling, we show that to reach its full potential, semantic role labeling systems need to incorporate language-specific features that do not easily apply across languages.

Chinese has a number of language-specific properties that factor into the formulation of the semantic role labeling problem. Compared to languages like Japanese and Czech, Chinese is morphology-poor. This can have both advantages and disadvantages. For example, there is no systematic use of morphological case markers, which would be useful cues for semantic role labeling. This also makes it impractical to use the Japanese-style semantic role labels that are essentially named after case markers. However, a benefit of impoverished morphology is that verbs and their nominalizations share the same morphological and orthographical forms, and this makes it easier to exploit the connections between verbal and nominal predicates. A second property is that Chinese tends to use a larger number of verbs than English, and the tradeoff is that Chinese verbs tend to be less polysemous. The larger verb vocabulary means smaller average verb frequency given a similar-sized corpus, and this means verbs that are seen in the training data are often absent in the test data. We describe a way to remedy this by using automatically derived verb classes. A third property is that Chinese words consist of characters rather than letters. Unlike letters that form English words, the majority of Chinese characters are morphemes that can also be words themselves in some context. Multi-character words are mostly compounds, and this is especially true for verbal predicates where verb components are sometimes incorporated arguments (e.g., 发 "hair" in 理发 "cut-hair") or predicates that have their own argument structures. Information encoded in verb components can thus be used to predict the argument structure of a compound verb. For example, if a verb has an incorporated object, it is unlikely that is will also have an external object. Finally, Chinese also has some syntactic constructions that do not have a close parallel in English, and they can be exploited to improve Chinese semantic role labeling. We describe semantic role labeling systems for both verbs and nouns, and we discuss how the language-specific properties can be exploited to improve Chinese semantic role labeling accuracy.

4.3.1   THE CHINESE PROPBANK

Most Chinese semantic role labeling research uses the Chinese PropBank (Xue and Palmer, 2009) as training and test data. The Chinese PropBank is the first large-scale Chinese corpus annotated with semantic roles, and it is developed in close association with the English Propbank (Palmer et al., 2005). Like the English Propbank, the Chinese Propbank distinguishes two different kinds of semantic roles for *core* and *adjunctive* arguments. The core arguments are marked with predicate-specific semantic roles *Arg0* through *Arg5*, and the adjunctive semantic roles are listed in Table 4.1. Most of these adjunctive semantic roles are similar to those in the English Propbank, but some of them need further elaboration. In particular, *TPC* is used to label topics, which is a notion that figures prominently in Chinese syntax (Li and Thompson, 1981). However, the TPC role in the Chinese Propbank is more of a semantic notion and is narrower than what it is generally assumed in syntax. Topic as a syntactic notion is mostly defined in structural terms and refers to a syntactic position in a syntactic parse tree. In Chinese, a topic can either be "base-generated" or moved to the topic position from its canonical position. Typically, an argument that is moved to the topic position is a core argument to a predicate in the sentence and is labeled with a numbered argument. Only the topics that are "base-generated" are labeled *TPC* in the Chinese Propbank.

Table 4.1: The complete list of functional tags defined in the Chinese Propbank			
ADV	adverbial	FRQ	frequency
BNF	beneficiary	LOC	locative
CND	condition	MNR	manner
DIR	direction	PRP	purpose or reason
DIS	discourse marker	TMP	temporal
DGR	degree	TPC	topic
EXT	extent		

Also like the English Propbank, the semantic role labels are assigned to constituents in a phrase structure tree as another layer of linguistic representation, as illustrated in (22). Although in most cases, there is a one-to-one correspondence between the constituent and the semantic role, there are also cases where multiple constituents in a parse tree receive the same label. Conversely, there are also cases where one constituent receives multiple semantic roles from different predicates. There are two scenarios when multiple constituents are assigned the same semantic role. One is when an argument is a trace which is linked to other constituents to form a chain. In this case, all constituents in that chain are assigned the same semantic role. The other scenario is when there is a discontinuous argument where multiple constituents jointly play a role with respect to a predicate. A constituent in a parse tree receives multiple semantic roles when there is *argument sharing* where this constituent plays a role for multiple predicates. This can happen in a coordination structure when multiple predicates are conjoined and share a subject. This can also happen in subject control or object control structures when two verbs share a subject or an object.

(22)

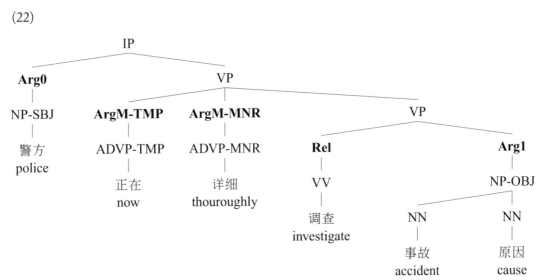

"The police are thoroughly investigating the cause of the accident."

4.3.2   SEMANTIC ROLE LABELING FOR VERBS

Commonalities   Like English semantic role labeling, Chinese semantic role labeling can be formulated as a classification task with three distinct stages: pruning, argument identification, and argument classification. The pruning algorithm described in Chapter 3 turns out to be straightforward to implement for Chinese data, and it involves minor changes in the phrase labels. For example, *IP* in the Chinese Treebank corresponds roughly to *S* in the Penn Treebank, and *CP* corresponds roughly to *SBAR*. Example 23 illustrates how the pruning algorithm works for Chinese. Assuming the predicate of interest is 调查 ("investigate"), the algorithm first adds the NP (事故 "accident" 原因 "cause") to the list of candidates. Then it moves up a level and adds the two ADVPs (正在 "now" and 详细 "thoroughly") to the list of candidates. At the next level, the two VPs form a coordination structure and thus no candidate is added. Finally, at the next level, the NP (警方 "police") is added to the list of candidates. Obviously, the pruning algorithm works better when the parse trees that are the input to the semantic role labeling system are correct. In a realistic scenario, the parse trees are generated by a syntactic parser and are not expected to be perfect. However, experimental results show that even when the parses are imperfect, using a pruning algorithm leads to an improvement in the overall semantic role labeling accuracy.

(23)

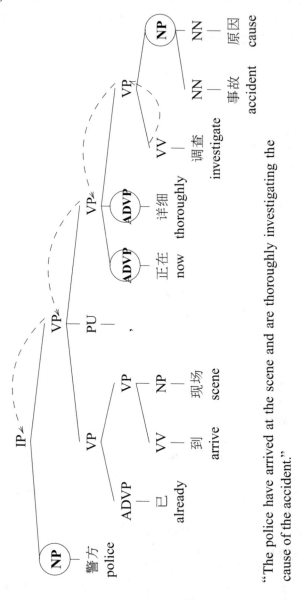

Most of the features that work well for English are also effective for Chinese. For example, Xue (2008) shows that using the Maximum Entropy model, his system produces a very strong baseline using the features that have been used in the English semantic role labeling literature.

The following is list of features that all made a positive impact on semantic role labeling for both Chinese and English. These features are ported directly from English semantic role labeling systems: Gildea and Jurafsky (2002), Xue and Palmer (2004) and Pradhan et al. (2004). Features marked "D" are for the binary classification of whether a constituent is an argument or not, while features marked "C" are for determining the specific semantic role of an argument:

I. **Features ported from English:**

C *Position*: The position is defined in relation to the predicate verb and the values are *before* and *after* (G&J)

C *Subcat frame*: The rule that expands the parent of the verb, e.g., *VP-> VV+NP* (G&J)

C *Phrase type*: The syntactic category of the constituent in focus, e.g., *NP, PP* (G&J)

C *First and last word of the constituent in focus* (P et al)

C *Phrase type of the sibling to the left* (P et al)

C *Subcat frame+*: The subcat frame that consists of the NPs that surround the predicate verb. This feature is defined by the position of the constituent in focus in relation to this syntactic frame (X&P)

C,D *Predicate*: The verb itself (G&J)

C,D *Path*: The path between the constituent in focus and the predicate. (G&J)

C,D *Head word and its part of speech*: The head word and its part-of-speech are often good indicators of the semantic role of a constituent. (G&J)

C,D *Combination features*: predicate-head word combination, predicate-phrase type combination. (X&P)

Chinese-specific features   The strong baseline for Chinese semantic role labeling achieved using just features for English suggests there is certain degree of similarity in the way that the arguments of Chinese and English verbs are realized in syntax; nevertheless, there are still areas where the two languages are different. For example, there is a BA construction in Chinese that does not have a close parallel in English. In the Chinese Treebank (Xue et al., 2005), the BA construction is identifiable by a closed class of words POS-tagged BA. Syntactically, BA is treated as a light verb that takes a clausal complement, and the subject of the clausal complement tends to be *Arg1* instead of *Arg0*, different from a typical clause or sentence in Chinese. Xue (2008) captures this information by using features describing the path from the light verb BA to the constituent in question. For example, the path from BA to the encircled NP in (24) is BA↑VP↓IP↓NP.

(24)

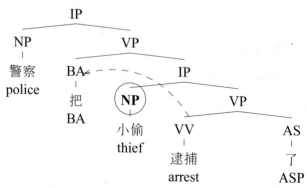

"The police arrested the thief."

Another syntactic construction in which the arguments are not realized in a canonical manner is the BEI construction. The BEI construction is the Chinese passive construction. However, unlike English, the BEI construction is not marked by passive morphology (past participle). Instead, the BEI construction is identifiable by a closed group of light verbs POS-tagged LB (for long BEI) and SB (for short BEI). LB takes a clausal complement while SB takes a verb phrase as a complement. In each case, the subject of NP is typically *Arg1* rather *Arg0*, as is the typical subject of a canonical clause in Chinese. In Xue (2008), this information is captured by the path from the light verb BEI to the constituent in question. For example, the path from BEI to the encircled NP in (25) is BEI↑VP↑IP↓NP.

(25)

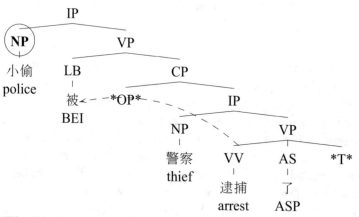

"The thief was arrested by the police."

Verb classes   Another major difference between Chinese and English as reflected in the English and Chinese Propbanks is that Chinese tends to use a much larger number of verbs. There are several reasons for this. One is that Chinese has so-called "stative verbs" that are generally translated into adjectives in English. That is, to convey the same meaning, English uses adjectives while Chinese uses stative verbs. The other reason is that Chinese verbs seem to be less polysemous than English verbs. The tradeoff is that Chinese seems to be using a larger verb vocabulary than English. One piece of evidence in support of this observation is that in the one-million-word Wall Street Journal section of the Penn Treebank (Marcus et al., 1993), there are about 4,000 verbs. The Chinese Treebank is a corpus that is slightly smaller in size, but it has over 15,000 verbs. The degree of polysemy versus the vocabulary size tradeoff cuts both ways for semantic role labeling. On the one hand, less polysemy usually means more uniform argument structure for verbs, which makes the semantic role labeling task easier. On the other hand, the larger vocabulary size increases the possibility that a given verb can only be found in the training data or test data but not both, thus exacerbating the data sparseness problem for machine learning algorithms. Xue (2008) addresses this by deriving a verb classification from the frame files that are created to guide the Chinese Propbank annotation so that if a verb is unseen in the training data, the machine learning algorithm can back off to the verb class for that verb and thus alleviate the sparse data problem.

Xue (2008) proposed a verb classification scheme based on three dimensions: the number of core arguments, the number of framesets, and syntactic alternation patterns. The first two dimensions can be extracted from the frame files fully automatically: the frame files are stored in XML format and the number of core arguments and the number of framesets can be obtained by parsing the frame files. The alternation patterns need to be manually added. The goal of this classification scheme is to put those verbs that have arguments realized in similar syntactic patterns in the same class. This maximizes the predictive power of the classes with respect to how the verb arguments are realized. A verb classification scheme derived in this manner may or may not have any semantic standing. That is, verbs in the same verb class may or may not be similar in meaning, but for semantic role labeling purposes, what is important is that their arguments are realized in a similar way providing guidance to the machine learning algorithm in terms of what semantic role to assign to which argument.

- **Number of arguments** Verbs in the Chinese PropBank can have one to five arguments, with the majority of them having one, two or three arguments. Verbs with zero arguments are auxiliary verbs[2] like 必 ("will"), 得以 ("be able to"), 该 ("should"), 敢 ("dare"), 可 ("may"), 肯 ("be willing to"), 能 ("can"), 能够 ("can"), 须 ("must"), 应当 ("should") and some other light verbs. Verbs that have five arguments are change of state verbs like 延长 ("lengthen"), 缩短 ("shorten"), 降低 ("lower"), 提高 ("increase"), 扩大 ("enlarge"), 缩小 ("make smaller"). These verbs generally take as arguments a theme that undergoes the change of state, the original state, the new state, the range of the change, and the cause or agent that brings about the change.

[2]One could say that the argument of the auxiliary verbs is the entire proposition, but in this phase of the Chinese PropBank, auxiliary verbs are not annotated.

- **Number of framesets** A frameset roughly corresponds to a major sense. This information is used because it is common that the different framesets of a verb can have different numbers of arguments. For example, verbs like 平衡 ("balance") can be used either as a non-stative or a stative verb. When it is used as a non-stative verb, it takes two arguments, the thing or situation that is balanced, and the entity that maintains the balance. When it is used as a stative verb, it takes only a single argument.

- **Syntactic alternations** We also represent certain types of syntactic alternations. One salient type of syntactic alternation is the well-known "causative/inchoative" alternation described in detail in Levin (1993). Chinese verbs that demonstrate this alternation pattern include 出版 ("publish"). For example, 这 ("this") 本 (CL) 书 ("book") plays the same semantic role even though it is the subject in "这 /this 本 /CL 书 /book 出版 /publish 了 /AS" and the object in "这 /this 家 /CL 出版 /publishing 社 /house 出版 /publish 了 /ASP 这 /this 本 /CL 书 /book."

Thus, each verb will belong to a class with a symbol representing each of the three dimensions. For example, a given verb may belong to the class "C1C2a," which means that this verb has two framesets, with the first frameset having one argument and the second having two arguments. The "a" in the second frameset represents a type of syntactic alternation. Once such a classification is in place, it can be used for formulate features that can be fed into the machine learning algorithm. For example, the verb class itself can be used as a feature, invoked if a predicate is in this class. The verb class can also form combination features with other information, such as the verb class + head word combination and verb class + phrase type combination.

Word formation features   Sun et al. (2009) described a syntactic chunker-based Chinese semantic role labeling system that achieved very competitive results. The system used different variations of an SVM classifier and achieved an F-measure of 74.12% when gold standard segmentations and part-of-speech tags are used, which represents a 2% improvement over what is reported in (Xue, 2008). The system uses a fairly standard IOB (Inside, Outside, Beginning) representation for syntactic chunking, combined with semantic role labels, as illustrated in (26).

(26)

[B – ArgM – TMP 截止][I – ArgM – TMP 目前][B – Arg0 保险 公司]
      until   now   insurance company

[B – ArgM – ADV 已   ][B – Arg2 为][I – Arg2 三峡   ][I – Arg2 工程]
      already   for   Three Gorge   project

[B – V 提供   ][B – Arg1 保险 服务   ]
   provide   insurance service

"Until now, the insurance company has provided insurance services for the Three Gorge Project."

Most of the features for the classifier are fairly standard, and they represent information about the syntactic chunk being classified (e.g., chunk type), the verbal predicate (e.g., POS tag, verb class), and the relation between the syntactic chunk and the verbal predicate (e.g., path, distance). It is worth mentioning that Sun et al. (2009) used word formation information as features. Unlike English words, Chinese words are composed of characters, most of which are words themselves. To put it differently, most words are compounds whose components can constrain their external grammatical behavior. For example, in 理发 ("cut-hair"), 发 ("hair") is already incorporated into the verb itself, and it is impossible for 理发 to have an external object as well. Conversely, 成 ("become") in 建成 ("build-become") adds another argument that is the result of 建 ("build"), which by itself does not take such an argument. Knowing the grammatical/semantic relation between the two components will help predict the arguments for the verb as a whole. Using features that represent word formation information (e.g., the head, modifier, object, or complement string of a verb), the semantic role labeling system achieved modest gains. However, intuitively this is a promising avenue for further exploration.

The use of syntactic chunks vs. full parses as input is a tradeoff that needs to considered very carefully when developing a semantic role labeling system. Results in the literature are inconclusive as to which is the better approach, but the relative strengths and weaknesses of the two approaches are not difficult to understand. Full parses have more structure and more fine-grained features can be defined on a full parse tree. For example, when defined on a parse tree, the *path* feature can clearly distinguish linguistic notions such as the subject and object, but given a chunk representation, the *path* can only be represented as a sequence of chunk or part-of-speech tags, deprived of the hierarchical information that is so useful in determining whether or not a constituent is an argument. Other full parse-based features such as subcat frames cannot be defined on a chunk representation at all. On the other hand, syntactic chunkers are generally more accurate than full syntactic parses. For example, the Chinese syntactic chunker used by Sun et al. (2009) in their work on semantic role labeling is comparable in accuracy to the state-of-the-art English syntactic chunkers, but the best Chinese syntactic parsers are still 5% to 10% lower in accuracy than state-of-the-art English parsers. If the syntactic parses are incorrect, the semantic role labeling system will not be able to extract the desired features or even the correct constituents to assign the semantic roles to. Some constituents will be prematurely excluded for consideration by the pruning algorithm or in the arguments identification. For this reason, using full syntactic parses tend to produce systems with high precision but low recall. Conversely, using syntactic chunks as input tend to include more argument candidates and thus raise the recall but lower the precision due to the lack of structural information.

4.3.3   SEMANTIC ROLE LABELING FOR NOUNS

So far our discussion has focused on the semantic role labeling of verbal predicates, as does most work on semantic role labeling. However, a large number of nouns are also predicates in the sense they denote relations among participants. Like the arguments for verbal predicates, the distribution of the arguments and adjuncts for nominalized predicates is not random, and they are located within a syntactic domain that can be defined with respect to the predicate. Compared with verbs, however, the distribution of the arguments for nominalized predicates is less uniform. There are two distinct ways in which the arguments of a nominalized predicate are realized, depending on the presence or absence of a support verb. The most common scenario in which a support verb is present is when the nominalized predicate heads an NP that is the syntactic object of this support verb. In this case, the arguments can be found both inside and outside the NP headed by the nominalized predicate, and the pruning algorithm works in a similar way as it does for verbs. The pruning algorithm starts from the nominalized predicate and collects its sisters. It then iteratively goes one level up until it reaches the top-level IP node. At each level, the sisters of the current node are added to the list of candidates. Note that the algorithm does not stop at the top NP level so that arguments outside the NP can also be captured. One issue that arises is what counts as a support verb. Linguistically support verbs are generally light verbs or semi-light verbs that have very little semantic content, but in practice, whether a verb is a support verb or not often depends on the context. Some verbs may be support verbs in some contexts but not in others. For example, "conduct" is a support verb in "conduct an investigation," but not a support verb in "conduct an opera." It is generally a good idea to err on the side of being overly inclusive and assuming that all verbs taking the NP headed by a nominalized predicate as its object are support verbs. This means adding constituents outside the NP as candidates when the NP is in the object position and letting the machine-learning algorithm figure out whether they are arguments or not. This pruning process is illustrated in (27), where the algorithm starts from the nominalized predicate 调查 ("investigation"). It first collects its sister ADJP (详细 "thorough"), and then it will go one level up to the NP, and add the support verb (进行 "conduct") to the candidate list. It will go another level up to the VP and adds its sisters ADVP (正在 "now") and PP (对 "toward" 事故 "accident" 原因 "cause") to the candidate list. It then goes one more level up and decides this is a coordination structure, and no candidate is added at this level. At the next VP level, it adds 警方 ("police") to the list of candidates. The algorithm terminates at the IP node.

(27)

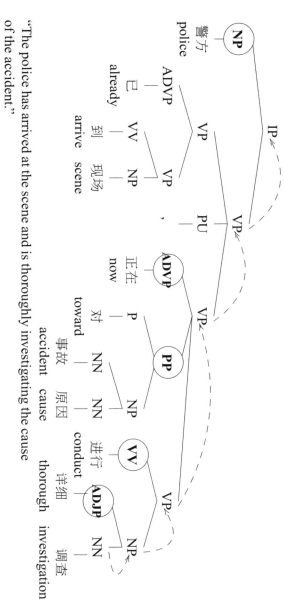

"The police has arrived at the scene and is thoroughly investigating the cause of the accident."

When the nominalized predicate does not occur with a support verb, generally all of its arguments are realized within the NP of which it is the head. In this case, there is little reason to include the constituents outside the NP. The pruning algorithm starts from the predicate, collects its sisters and adds them to the candidate list. It then iteratively goes up one level and collects the sisters of that constituent until it reaches the top-level NP of which it is the head. An exception is made when the constituent is DNP, in which case the candidate added is the first daughter of the DNP, not the DNP itself. This is illustrated in (28), where the algorithm starts from the nominalized predicate 调查 ("investigation"), and since it does not have any sisters, it does not add anything to the candidate list at this level. It then goes up to its parent NP and collects its sisters NP (警方 "police") and DNP (对 "toward" 事故 "accident" 原因 "cause" 的 "DE"). In the case of DNP, the candidate added is actually its first daughter, the PP.

(28)

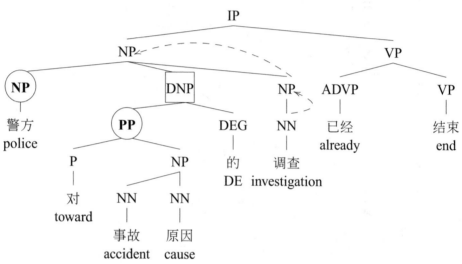

"The police investigation of the cause of the accident has ended."

Overall, Xue (2008) shows that pruning works less effectively for nouns than for verbs, as expected. However, using the pruning algorithm still improves the overall semantic role labeling accuracy, and this is true for all experimental conditions whether treebank parses or automatic parses are used as input. There is a small drop in recall as a result of the pruning algorithm, which is more than offset by the gain in precision.

Feature adaption   When moving from verbal to nominalized predicates, the features for a semantic role labeling system have to be adapted as well. Some features that are designed for verbal predicates may not readily carry over to nominalized predicates. For example, it is not obvious how the subcat feature and the subcat+ features can be defined for nominalized predicates. The BA and BEI features are also specific to syntactic constructions projected by verbs and have no relevance to nominalized predicates. In the mean time, there are other features that are specific to nominalized predicates that need to be added. For example, a support verb to a large extent determines whether or not the arguments of a nominalized predicate can occur outside the NP of which it is the head. Therefore, it is effective information for discriminating arguments from non-arguments. It is also indicative of the specific semantic role of an argument, and, therefore, useful for argument classification as well. Xue (2008) captures this information with a combined feature of path + governing verb that was only invoked when there was an intervening governing verb between the constituent being classified and the predicate. The governing verb is used as an approximation of the support verb for this feature because the system does not have prior knowledge of whether a verb is a support verb or not absent some external resource that provides a list of possible support verbs. The governing verb, on the other hand, can be approximated by looking at the syntactic configuration between the nominalized predicate and the verb. This feature is used for both argument detection and argument classification. Unlike verbs which project well-defined syntactic positions such as subject and object, arguments of a nominalized predicate tend to be syntactic modifiers of the predicate in a flat NP structure. Xue (2008) captures this information using a sisterhood feature that indicates whether the constituent being classified is a sister to the nominalized predicate. The sisterhood feature is used for both argument detection and argument classification. In addition, Xue (2008) shows that there are three additional features that are useful specifically for detecting arguments for nominalized predicates. When a nominalized predicate is in the subject position, the NP in the topic position tends to be its argument. A binary feature is invoked when the constituent in focus is an NP that is the left sister of the subject NP headed by the predicate. Whether an NP is a subject is also determined heuristically: an NP is considered to be a subject if its parent is an IP and its right sister is a VP. Another binary feature used for argument detection is whether the constituent in focus is inside the NP headed by the predicate. Finally, the position of the constituent in relation to the support verb is also used as a feature for argument detection. The values for this feature can be before or after the support verb or can be the support verb itself. The full list of features used for semantic role labeling of nominalized predicates in Chinese are listed below:

I. **Baseline Features:**

C *Position*: The position is defined in relation to the predicate and the values are *before* and *after*. Since most of the arguments for nominalized predicates in Chinese are before the predicates, this feature is not as discriminative as when it is used for verbal predicates where arguments can be both before or after the predicate. (G&J)

C *Phrase type*: The syntactic category of the constituent being classified. (G&J)

C *First and last word of the constituent being classified.* (P et al)

C,D *Predicate*: The nominalized predicate itself. (G&J)

C,D *Predicate combination features*: Predicate - head word combination, predicate - phrase type combination (X&P)

C,D *Predicate class*: The verb class the predicate belongs to. Same predicate class as those used for verbs

C,D *Predicate class combination features.* predicate class + head combination, predicate class + phrase type combination

C,D *Head word and its part of speech*: The head word and its part-of-speech. (G&J)

C,D *Path*: The path between the constituent being classified and the predicate (G&J)

II. **Adapted features:**

C,D *Path*: The path between the constituent being classified and the predicate, with the predicate clearly identified.

III. **New Features:**

D *Topic NP*: A binary feature indicating whether the constituent is a topic if the predicate is the subject

D *Inside NP headed by the predicate*: A binary feature indicating whether the constituent in focus is inside the NP headed by the predicate

D *Position of the constituent in relation to the support verb*: the value can be before, after the support verb, or is the support verb itself.

C,D *Sisterhood with predicate*: A binary feature that indicates whether the constituent is a sister to the predicate

C,D *Path + governing verb.* The path feature combined with the governing verb.

Incorporating features from verbal SRL   One salient morphological/orthographical characteristic of the Chinese language is that Chinese nominalization involves "zero" conversion. That is, verbs and their nominalized forms are orthographically the same words. One obvious way to exploit this linguistic property would be to train a unified model for both verbal and nominal semantic role labeling. Xue and Palmer (2005) show that this simplistic approach does not work well, and adding verb instances to enhance the training data for nominalized predicates hurt the SRL accuracy for nouns instead of improving it. This result is hardly surprising upon closer examination. While verbs and their nominalizations share the same morphological/orthographic forms, the syntactic realizations of their arguments are very different. With the majority of predicates having all of their arguments realized within the NP they project, the same feature template may extract very different information for nominal and verbal predicates. The path feature, for example, will have very different values when the predicate is a verb or a noun. This is not to say, however, that nominal SRL cannot benefit from verbal SRL in any way. In more recent work on Chinese nominal SRL, Li et al. (2009) show that features extracted from the *output* of a verbal SRL system helps improve nominal SRL accuracy. Instead of simply adding manually annotated verb instances to nouns as training data, and effectively training one unified system, Li et al. developed a verbal SRL system first and then used the output of the verbal system to improve the nominal SRL accuracy. These features take advantage of an inherent connection between the nominalized predicate and its support verb. For example, in (27), The NP 警方 ("police") is annotated as *Arg0* for both the nominal predicate 调查 ("investigation") and the support verb '进行 ("conduct"). In addition, the NP headed by the nominal predicate 详细 调查 ("careful investigation") is annotated as *Arg1* of the support verb. The semantic role labels produced by the verbal SRL system can be used to predict the semantic role of the nominal predicate. Li et al. defined the following features from the output of a verbal SRL system:

- Whether the constituent under consideration is an argument for the support verb as well (yes or no)

- The semantic role of the constituent for the support verb

- Whether the NP headed by the nominal predicate is an argument of the support verb (yes or no)

- The semantic role of this NP

There is far less research in semantic role labeling on nouns than verbs in general. For some discussion on English semantic role labeling, see Pradhan et al. (2004) and Jiang and Ng (2006).

4.3.4   SUMMARY

The lesson learned from the collective experience of developing Chinese and English semantic role labeling systems is that, while the general approach of formulating semantic role labeling as a classification problem is effective and many features described in the semantic role labeling literature port well between the two languages, careful attention needs to paid to language-specific properties for semantic role labeling to reach its full potential for a particular language. Language independent techniques can only carry us so far. As semantic role labeling is only starting to flourish in a multilingual context, any conclusion we draw here is necessarily preliminary. The features that work well for both English and Chinese may not be equally effective in a third language. For languages that have a dependency-based grammatical tradition, many of the features may not apply at all.

EXERCISES

1. Obtain parallel bilingual text for a language pair you are familiar with, and annotate predicate-argument structures for all verbs in small amount of text. Assuming that one of the languages is English, you may use the PropBank frame files as a guideline for the English argument structure; define frames and semantic roles for verbs in the other language as you proceed. How often do the argument structures in the two languages coincide? Do you observe any general differences between the languages?

2. If your native language or a language you are familiar with does not yet have manual semantic role annotation, but there exists parallel data between that language and English, implement a semantic role projection system that transfers semantic roles from English to that language. How well does the semantic role projection work between those two languages?

3. If there is a parallel corpus with semantic role annotation on both sides, and you are familiar with both the source and the target language, try to evaluate how well semantic roles transfer by implementing the semantic role alignment algorithm described in the chapter. Extract all instances where different semantic role labels are used. Are the semantic role mismatches genuine, in the sense that they have different role definitions, or are they just different labels describing the same role?

4. Develop a semantic role labeling system for a language that you know and where manual semantic role annotation is available. How does the semantic role labeling accuracy for that language compare to English and Chinese? Are there language-specific properties that you can exploit as features?

CHAPTER 5

Summary

The preceding chapters have described several aspects of semantic role labeling. We began with a description of semantic role labels and various linguistic theories that make claims about different types of labels. We presented several different lexical resources, FrameNet, VerbNet and PropBank, specifically designed to provide semantic role labels for individual senses of verbs and other parts of speech. These resources are also associated with annotated corpora which can be used as training data for supervised machine learning. We then moved on to a discussion of the use of machine learning to build systems that automatically assign semantic role labels to previously unseen sentences. This involved a discussion of the stages of the processing, the choice of features, different types of classifiers, and the use of joint inference to take advantage of context sensitivities. We also explored the impact of syntactic parsing on semantic role labeling, describing efforts to integrate syntactic parsing with semantic role labeling, and the use of different syntactic representations individually or collectively to improve semantic role labeling accuracy. Another line of research that was discussed is the study of the impact of different styles of semantic role labels on system accuracy. Finally, we discussed unsupervised and partially supervised approaches to semantic role labeling.

While there has been a rapid accumulation of research on the English language in less than ten years, semantic role labeling in a multilingual context is still an emerging field. Statistical machine learning is the predominant approach for current semantic role labeling systems, which are trained on substantial amounts of manually annotated data like the corpora described in Chapter 2. We discussed efforts to circumvent this data bottleneck by projecting semantic role annotation from English to other languages via parallel data. We also presented a way of aligning predicate-argument structures where parallel propbanks are available. Finally, we discussed issues involved in building automatic semantic role labeling systems for other languages, with respect to both data annotation and system building.

Several conclusions can be drawn from this discussion of semantic role labeling. Certainly, the preparation of training data must be informed by linguistics. Having a clear understanding of the differences between Agents and Patients and their likely syntactic environments is central to the art of semantic role labeling. However, knowledge of linguistics is necessary but not sufficient; the preparation of useful training data also benefits from some understanding of the machine learning process and interactions between annotation choices and the resulting data. The semantic role classes need to have enough representative instances to avoid data sparseness, as illustrated by *Arg0* and *Arg1* for PropBank. However, it is also important that the classes be internally coherent and consistently labeled. PropBank's *Arg2* may have plenty of instances, but they are so diverse and occur in such a wide range of syntactic environments that machine learning algorithms fail to extract predictive features. Generalizations are good, but they must be consistent and predictable generalizations to benefit machine learning. It can also be useful for the system builder to understand the underlying linguistic theory well enough to decide whether or not it is worth having a separate Argument Identification Stage and to know how to most effectively climb the syntactic tree in search of predicate arguments. A linguistically informed system builder also has an advantage in choosing between different features or perhaps between different feature combinations. With respect to feature combinations, SVMs can automatically make choices for the system builder, but the same results can be achieved much more quickly by maximum entropy using manually selected, linguistically appropriate feature combinations. This is even more important when porting a system to another task such as nominalizations or to another language. Which features are likely to generalize to the new task, and which ones are not? Successful attempts to improve system performance based on joint inference were prompted by an understanding of the context-sensitive nature of semantic role labeling; individual role labels are not assigned independently of the other role labels for the same predicate, but they sing a chorus together in an harmonious fashion.

Is semantic role labeling (for English at least) effectively a solved problem or are there interesting new directions for semantic role labeling to go in the future? There are several promising avenues: breaking the glass ceiling of syntactic parsing performance through improved syntax/semantic interaction; improved robustness for English in new genres and new domains through better generalizations based on more effective utilization of the semantic links between PropBank, VerbNet and FrameNet which will lead to informed backoff to verb classes; the projection of semantic role labels onto parallel corpora to create training data for new languages; the linking together of individual predicate argument structures into complex event representations that include temporal and spatial information; the creation of richer semantic representations by associating inference rules with VerbNet and FrameNet semantic predicates; and, last but not least, developing semi-supervised and unsupervised approaches for all of these tasks.

Bibliography

Abeillé, Anne and Owen Rambow, (Eds.). 2001. *Tree Adjoining Grammars: Formalisms, Linguistic Analysis and Processing*. Center for the Study of Language and Information, Stanford, CA. 47

Baker, Collin F., Charles J. Fillmore, and John B. Lowe. 1998. The Berkeley FrameNet Project. In *Proceedings of the 17th International Conference on Computational Linguistics (COLING/ACL-98)*, pages 86–90, Montreal. ACL. DOI: 10.3115/980451.980860 18, 21, 54

Baker, Collin F. and Josef Ruppenhofer. 2002. FrameNet's Frames vs. Levin's Verb Classes. In *Proceedings of the 28th Annual Meeting of the Berkeley Linguistics Society*. 22

Bikel, Daniel M., Richard Schwartz, and Ralph M. Weischedel. 1999. An Algorithm that Learns What's in a Name. *Machine Learning*, 34:211–231. DOI: 10.1023/A:1007558221122 41

Burchardt, A., K. Erk, A. Frank, A. Kowalski, S. Padó, and M. Pinkal. 2006. The SALSA Corpus: a German Corpus Resource for Lexical Semantics. In *Proceedings of the Language Resources and Evaluation Conference (LREC-06)*, pages 969–974, Genoa, Italy. 53, 54

Carreras, Xavier and Lluís Màrquez. 2004. Introduction to the CoNLL-2004 Shared Task: Semantic Role Labeling. In *Proceedings of the Eighth Conference on Computational Natural Language Learning (CoNLL-04)*, pages 89–97. 46

Carreras, Xavier and Lluís Màrquez. 2005. Introduction to the CoNLL-2005 Shared Task: Semantic Role Labeling. In *Proceedings of the Ninth Conference on Computational Natural Language Learning (CoNLL-05)*. 46

Charniak, Eugene. 2000. A Maximum-Entropy-Inspired Parser. In *Proceedings of the 1st Annual Meeting of the North American Chapter of the ACL (NAACL-00)*, pages 132–139, Seattle, Washington. 1, 49

Charniak, Eugene and Mark Johnson. 2005. Coarse-to-Fine n-Best Parsing and Maxent Discriminative Reranking. In *Proceedings of the 43rd Annual Meeting of the Association for Computational Linguistics (ACL-05)* DOI: 10.3115/1219840.1219862 35, 46

Chen, John and Owen Rambow. 2003. Use of Deep Linguistic Features for the Recognition and Labeling of Semantic Arguments. In *Proceedings of the 2003 Conference on Empirical Methods in Natural Language Processing (EMNLP-03)*, pages 41–48. DOI: 10.3115/1119355.1119361 48

Choi, Jinho, Martha Palmer, and Nianwen Xue. 2009. Using Parallel PropBanks to Enhance Word-Alignments. In *Proceedings of the Third Linguistic Annotation Workshop*, held in conjunction with the *49th Annual Meeting of the Association for Computational Linguistics (ACL-2009)*, pages 121–124, Suntec, Singapore, August. 61

Chomsky, Noam. 1982. *Lectures on Government and Binding: The Pisa Lectures*. Foris Publications, Dordrecht, Holland. 6

Collins, Michael. 1997. Three Generative, Lexicalised Models for Statistical Parsing. In *Proceedings of the 35th Annual Meeting of the Association for Computational Linguistics (ACL-97)*, pages 16–23, Madrid, Spain. DOI: 10.3115/976909.979620 33, 35, 40

Collins, Michael. 2000. Discriminative Reranking for Natural Language Parsing. In *Machine Learning: Proceedings of the Seventeenth International Conference (ICML-00)*, pages 175–182, Stanford, California. DOI: 10.1162/0891201053630273 1

Collins, Michael John. 1999. *Head-driven Statistical Models for Natural Language Parsing*. Ph.D. thesis, University of Pennsylvania, Philadelphia. DOI: 10.1162/089120103322753356 40, 46, 47

Cruse, D. A., (Ed.). 1973. *Lexical Semantics*. Cambridge University Press, Cambridge, England. 6

Dang, Hoa Trang, Karin Kipper, Martha Palmer, and Joseph Rosenzweig. 1998. Investigating Regular Sense Extensions Based on Intersective Levin Classes. In *Proceedings of the 17th International Conference on Computational Linguistics (COLING/ACL-98)*, pages 293–299, Montreal. ACL. DOI: 10.3115/980451.980893 18, 22

Diab, Mona, Alessadro Moschitti, and Daniele Phghin. 2008. Semantic Role Labeling Systems for Arabic Language Using Kernel Methods. In *Proceedings of the 46th Annual Meeting of the Association for Computational Linguistics (ACL-08)*, Columbus, Ohio. 53

Dienes, Peter and Amit Dubey. 2003. Antecedent Recovery: Experiments with a Trace Tagger. In *Proceedings of the 2003 Conference on Empirical Methods in Natural Language Processing (EMNLP-03)*, Sapporo, Japan. DOI: 10.3115/1119355.1119360 37

Dorr, Bonnie J. 1994. Machine Translation Divergences: A Formal Description and Proposed Solution. *Computational Linguistics*, 20(4):597–633. 9

Dorr, Bonnie J. and Douglas Jones. Acquisition of Semantic Lexicons: Using Word Sense Disambiguation to Improve Precision, in Evelyn Viegas (Ed.), Breadth and Depth of Semantic Lexicons, Kluwer Academic Publishers, Norwell, MA, pp. 79–98, 2000. 22

Dorr, Bonnie J. and Clare R. Voss. 1996. A Multi-Level Approach to Interlingual MT: Defining the Interface Between Representational Languages. *International Journal of Expert Systems*, 9(1):15–51. 9

Dowty, David. 2003. The Dual Analysis of Adjuncts and Complements in Categorial Grammar. In Ewald Lang, Claudia Maienborn, and Catherine Fabricius-Hansen, (Eds.), *Modifying Adjuncts*. de Gruyter, Berlin - New York, pages 1–22. 8

Dowty, David R. 1991. Thematic Proto-Roles and Argument Selection. *Language*, 67(3):547–619. DOI: 10.2307/415037 7, 10, 13

Ellsworth, Michael, Katrin Erk, Paul Kingsbury, and Sebastian Padó. 2004. PropBank, Salsa, and FrameNet: How Design Determines Product. In *LREC 2004 Workshop on Building Lexical Resources from Semantically Annotated Corpora*, Lisbon, Portugal. 25

Fillmore, Charles J. 1968. The Case for Case. In Emmon W. Bach and Robert T. Harms, (Eds.), *Universals in Linguistic Theory*. Holt, Rinehart & Winston, New York, pages 1–88. 2

Fillmore, Charles J. 1982. Frame Semantics. In *Linguistics in the Morning Calm*. Hanshin, Seoul, pages 111–138. Linguistics Society of Korea. 18

Fillmore, Charles J. 1985. Frames and the Semantics of Understanding. *Quaderni di Semantica*, VI(2):222–254. 7, 18

Fillmore, Charles J., Christopher R. Johnson, and Miriam R.L. Petruck. 2002. Background to FrameNet. *International Journal of Lexicography*, 16(3):2435–250. DOI: 10.1093/ijl/16.3.235 18

Fleischman, Michael, Namhee Kwon, and Edward Hovy. 2003. Maximum Entropy Models for FrameNet Classification. In *Proceedings of the 2003 Conference on Empirical Methods in Natural Language Processing (EMNLP-03)*, Sapporo, Japan. DOI: 10.3115/1119355.1119362 41, 43, 45

Fung, Pascale, Zhaojun Wu, Yongsheng Yang, and Dekai Wu. 2007. Learning Bilingual Semantic Frames: Shallow Semantic Parsing vs. Semantic Role Projection. In *Proceedings of the 11th Conference on Theoretical and Methodological Issues in Machine Translation (TMI-07)*, pages 75–84, Skövde, Sweden. 56, 59

Fürstenau, Hagen and Mirella Lapata. 2009. Semi-Supervised Semantic Role Labeling. In *Proceedings of the European Chapter of the ACL (EACL-09)*, pages 220–228. 51

Gabbard, Ryan, Mitchell Marcus, and Seth Kulick. 2006. Fully Parsing the Penn TreeBank. In *Proceedings of Human Language Technology Conference of the North American Chapter of the Association of Computational Linguistics (NAACL-06)*, pages 184–191. DOI: 10.3115/1220835.1220859 37

Gildea, Daniel and Julia Hockenmaier. 2003. Identifying Semantic Roles Using Combinatory Categorial Grammar. In *Proceedings of the 2003 Conference on Empirical Methods in Natural Language Processing (EMNLP-2003)*, pages 57–64, Sapporo, Japan. DOI: 10.3115/1119355.1119363 48

Gildea, Daniel and Daniel Jurafsky. 2002. Automatic Labeling for Semantic Roles. *Computational Linguistics*, 28(3):245–288. DOI: 10.1162/089120102760275983 32, 33, 35, 36, 39, 41, 43, 44, 47, 65

Giuglea, Ana-Maria and Alessandro Moschitti. 2006. Semantic Role Labeling Via FrameNet, Verb-Net and PropBank. In *Proceedings of the 21st International Conference on Computational Linguistics and 44th Annual Meeting of the Association for Computational Linguistics (COLING/ACL-06)*, pages 929–936, Sydney, Australia. DOI: 10.3115/1220175.1220292 50, 51

Gordon, Andrew and Reid Swanson. 2007. Generalizing Semantic Role Annotations Across Syntactically Similar Verbs. In *Proceedings of the 45th Annual Meeting of the Association for Computational Linguistics (ACL-07)*. 51

Grenager, Trond and Christopher Manning. 2006. Unsupervised Discovery of a Statistical Verb Lexicon. In *Proceedings of the 2006 Conference on Empirical Methods in Natural Language Processing (EMNLP-06)*, pages 1–8. 52

Gruber, Jeffrey S. 1965. *Studies in Lexical Relations*. Ph.D. thesis, MIT, Cambridge, MA. 7

Alena Böhmová, Hajič, Jan, Eva Hajicová, and Barbora Hladká. 2003. The PDT: A Three Level Annotation Scenario. In Anne Abeillé, (Ed.), *TreeBanks: Building and Using Annotated Corpora*. Kluwer Academic Publishers. 53, 55

Hockenmaier, Julia and Mark Steedman. 2002. Generative Models for Statistical Parsing with Combinatory Categorial Grammar. In *Proceedings of the 40th Annual Meeting of the Association for Computational Linguistics (ACL-02)*, Philadelphia, PA. DOI: 10.3115/1073083.1073139 48

Hofmann, Thomas and Jan Puzicha. 1998. Statistical Models for Co-Occurrence Data. Memo, Massachusetts Institute of Technology Artificial Intelligence Laboratory, February. 42

Jackendoff, Ray. 1972. *Semantic Interpretation in Generative Grammar*. MIT Press, Cambridge, Massachusetts. 5, 7

Jackendoff, Ray. 1983. *Semantics and Cognition*. MIT Press, Cambridge, Mass. 6, 7

Jackendoff, Ray. 1992. *Semantic Structures*. MIT Press, Cambridge, Mass. 9

Jiang, Zheng Ping and Hwee Tou Ng. 2006. Semantic Role Labeling of NomBank: A Maximum Entropy Approach. In *Proceedings of the 2006 Conference on Empirical Methods in Natural Language Processing (EMNLP-06)*, pages 138–145, Sydney, Australia, July. 75

Johansson, Richard and Pierre Nugues. 2006. A FrameNet-Based Semantic Role Labeler for Swedish. In *Proceedings of the COLING/ACL 2006 Main Conference Poster Sessions*, pages 436–443, Sydney, Australia, July. Association for Computational Linguistics. 56, 57

Johansson, Richard and Pierre Nugues. 2008. Dependency-Based Semantic Role Labeling of PropBank. In *Proceedings of the 2008 Conference on Empirical Methods in Natural Language Processing (EMNLP-08)*, pages 69–78. 48

Johnson, Christopher R., Charles J. Fillmore, Esther J. Wood, Josef Ruppenhofer, Margaret Urban, Miriam R. L. Petruck, and Collin F. Baker. 2001. The FrameNet Project: Tools for Lexicon Building. Version 0.7, `http://ccl.pku.edu.cn/doubtfire/semantics/FrameNet/` `theory/FrameNet_book.pdf` 18, 21

Johnson, Mark. 2002. A Simple Pattern-Matching Algorithm for Recovering Empty Nodes and Their Antecedents. In *Proceedings of the 40th Annual Meeting of the Association for Computational Linguistics (ACL-02)*, Philadelphia, PA. DOI: 10.3115/1073083.1073107 37

Joshi, A. K., L. S. Levy, and M. Takahashi. 1975. Tree Adjunct Grammars. *Journal of Computer and System Sciences*, 10:136–163. 47

Katz, Slava M. 1987. Estimation of Probabilities from Sparse Data for the Language Model Component of Speech Recognition. *IEEE Transactions on Acoustics, Speech, and Signal Processing*, 35:400–401. DOI: 10.1109/TASSP.1987.1165125 43

Kawahara, Daisuke, Sadao Kurohashi, and Koichi Hashida. 2002. Construction of a Japanese Relevance-Tagged Corpus (in Japanese). In *Proceedings of the 8th Annual Meeting of the Association for Natural Language Processing*, pages 495–498. 55

Kipper, Karin, Hoa Trang Dang, and Martha Palmer. 2000. Class-Based Construction of a Verb Lexicon. In *Proceedings of the Seventeenth National Conference on Artificial Intelligence (AAAI-00)*, Austin, TX, July-August. 18, 51

Kipper, Karin, Hoa Trang Dang, William Schuler, and Martha Palmer. 2000. Building a Class-Based Verb Lexicon Using TAGs. In *Fifth International Workshop on Tree Adjoining Grammars and Related Formalisms (TAG+5)*, pages 147–154, Paris, May. 22

Kipper, Karin, Anna Korhonen, Neville Ryant, and Martha Palmer. 2008. A Large-Scale Classification of English Verbs. *Language Resources and Evaluation Journal*, 42(1):21–40. DOI: 10.1007/s10579-007-9048-2 22

Kipper Schuler, Karin. 2005. *VerbNet: A Broad-Coverage, Comprehensive Verb Lexicon*. Ph.D. thesis, University of Pennsylvania. 22, 51

Korhonen, Anna and Ted Briscoe. 2004. Extended Lexical-Semantic Classification of English Verbs. In *Proceedings of HLT/NAACL Workshop on Computational Lexical Semantics*, Boston, Mass. ACL. 23

Korhonen, Anna, Yuval Krymolowski, and Zvika Marx. 2003. Clustering Polysemic Subcategorization Frame Distributions Semantically. In *Proceedings of the 41st Annual Meeting of the Association for Computational Linguistics (ACL-03)*, Sapporo, Japan, pages 64–71. 22

Kučera, Henry and W. Nelson Francis. 1967. *Computational Analysis of Present-Day American English*. Brown University Press, Providence, RI. 50

Kwon, Namhee, Michael Fleischman, and Eduard Hovy. 2004. Senseval Automatic Labeling of Semantic Roles Using Maximum Entropy Models. In *Third International Workshop on the Evaluation of Systems for the Semantic Analysis of Text (Senseval-3)*, pages 129–132, Barcelona, Spain, July. 50

Lakoff, George. 1987. *Women, Fire, and Dangerous Things: What Categories Reveal About the Mind.* University of Chicago Press, Chicago, Ill. 10

Levin, Beth. 1993. *English Verb Classes And Alternations: A Preliminary Investigation.* University of Chicago Press, Chicago. 7, 14, 42, 68

Li, Charles and Sandra Thompson. 1981. *Mandarin Chinese: A Functional Reference Grammar.* Berkeley, Los Angeles, London: University of California Press. 62

Li, Junhui, Guodong Zhou, Hai Zhao, Qiaoming Zhu, and Peide Qian. 2009. Improving Nominal SRL in Chinese Language With Verbal SRL Information and Automatic Predicate Recognition. In *Proceedings of the 2009 Conference on Empirical Methods in Natural Language Processing (EMNLP-09)*, pages 1280–1288, Singapore, August. 74

Lida, Ryu, Mamoru Komachi, Kentaro Inui, and Yuji Matsumoto. 2007. Annotating a Japanese Text Corpus With a Predicate-Argument and Coreference Relations. In *Proceedings of the 1st Linguistic Annotation Workshop*, pages 132–139. 53, 55

Lin, Dekang. 1998. Dependency-Based Evaluation of Minipar. In *Workshop on the Evaluation of Parsing Systems*, Granada, Spain. 49

Litkowski, Ken. 2004. Senseval-3 task: Automatic Labeling of Semantic Roles. In *Third International Workshop on the Evaluation of Systems for the Semantic Analysis of Text (Senseval-3)*, pages 9–12, Barcelona, Spain, July. 50

Loper, Edward, Szu-ting Yi, and Martha Palmer. 2007. Combining Lexical Resources: Mapping Between PropBank and VerbNet. In the *Proceedings of the 7th International Workshop on Computational Semantics*, Tilburg, the Netherlands. 28

Marcus, Mitchell P., Grace Kim, Mary Ann Marcinkiewicz, Robert MacIntyre, Ann Bies, Mark Ferguson, Karen Katz, and Britta Schasberger. 1994. The Penn TreeBank: Annotating Predicate Argument Structure. In *ARPA Human Language Technology Workshop*, pages 114–119, Plainsboro, NJ. Morgan Kaufmann. 36

Marcus, Mitchell P., Beatrice Santorini, and Mary Ann Marcinkiewicz. 1993. Building a Large Annotated Corpus of English: The Penn TreeBank. *Computational Linguistics*, 19(2):313–330. 33, 67

McDonald, Ryan, Fernando Pereira, Kiril Ribarov, and Jan Hajič. 2005. Non-Projective Dependency Parsing Using Spanning Tree Algorithms. In *Proceedings of Human Language Technology Conference and Conference on Empirical Methods in Natural Language Processing (HLT/EMNLP-05)*. DOI: 10.3115/1220575.1220641 1, 48

Merlo, Paola and Gabriele Musillo. 2008. Semantic Parsing for High-Precision Semantic Role Labelling. In *Proceedings of the Twelfth Conference on Computational Natural Language Learning (CoNLL-08)*. 47

Merlo, Paola and Lonneke van der Plas. 2009. Abstraction and Generalisation in Semantic Role Labels: PropBank, VerbNet or both? In *Proceedings of the 47th Annual Meeting of the Association for Computational Linguistics (ACL-09)*. 51

Meyers, A., R. Reeves, C. Macleod, R. Szekely, V. Zielinska, B. Young, and R. Grishman. 2004. Annotating Noun Argument Structure for NomBank. In *Proceedings of the Language Resources and Evaluation Conference (LREC-04)*, Lisbon, Portugal. 21

Mikulová, Marie, Allevtina Bémová, Jan Hajič, Eva Hajičová, Jiři Havelka, Veronika Kolářová, Lucie Kučová, Markéta Lopatková, Petr Pajas, Jarmila Panevová, Magda Ševčíková, Petr Sgall, Jan ŠtěPánek, Zdeňka Urešová, Kateřina Veselá, and Zdeněk Žabokrtský. 2006. Charles University Technical Report. Annotation on the Tectogrammatical level in the Prague Dependency TreeBank: Reference Book. 55

Minsky, Marvin. 1975. A Framework for Representing Knowledge. In Patrick Henry Winston, (Ed.), *The Psychology of Computer Vision*. McGraw-Hill, NY, NY. DOI: 10.1016/0031-3203(76)90020-0 18

Nivre, J., J. Hall, and J. Nilsson. 2006. Maltparser: A Data-Driven Parser-Generator for Dependency Parsing. In *Proceedings of the Language Resources and Evaluation Conference (LREC-06)*, pages 2216–2219, Genoa, Italy. 1, 48

Och, Franz Josef and Hermann Ney. 2003. A Systematic Comparison of Various Statistical Alignment Models. *Computational Linguistics*, 29(1):19–51. DOI: 10.1162/089120103321337421 56

Ohara, Kyoko Hirose. 2008. Representing Lexicon and Grammar in Japanese FrameNet. In *Proceedings of the Fifth International Conference on Construction Grammar*, Austin, Texas. 53, 54

Padó, Sebastian. 2007. *Cross-Lingual Annotation Projection Models for Role-Semantic Information*. Ph.D. thesis, Saarland University. 59

Padó, Sebastian and Katrin Erk. 2005. To Cause or not to Cause: Cross-Lingual Semantic Matching for Paraphrase Modelling. In *Proceedings of the Cross-Language Knowledge Induction Workshop*, Cluj-Napoca, Romania. 59

Padó, Sebastian and Mirella Lapata. 2005. Cross-Linguistic Projection of Role-Semantic Information. In *Proceedings of Human Language Technology Conference and Conference on Empirical Methods
in Natural Language Processing (HLT/EMNLP-05)*, pages 859–866, Vancouver, British Columbia,
Canada. DOI: 10.3115/1220575.1220683 56, 58

Palmer, M., C. Weir, R. Passonneau, and T. Finin. 1993. The Kernel Text Understanding System. *Artificial Intelligence*, 63:17–68, October. Special Issue on Text Understanding.
DOI: 10.1016/0004-3702(93)90014-3 9

Palmer, Martha. 1990. *Semantic Processing for Finite Domains*. Cambridge University Press, Cambridge, England. 9

Palmer, Martha, Ann Bies, Olga Babko-Malaya, Mona Diab, Mohamed Maamouri, Aous Mansouri,
and Wajdi Zaghouni. 2008. A Pilot Arabic PropBank. In *Proceedings of the Language Resources
and Evaluation Conference (LREC-08)*, Marrakech, Morocco. 53, 54

Palmer, Martha, Daniel Gildea, and Paul Kingsbury. 2005. The Proposition Bank:
An Annotated Corpus of Semantic Roles. *Computational Linguistics*, 31(1):71–106.
DOI: 10.1162/0891201053630264 25, 54, 62

Palmer, Martha, Jena D. Hwang, Susan Windisch Brown, Karin Kipper Schuler, and Arrick Lan-
franchi. 2009. Leveraging Lexical Resources for the Detection of Event Relations. In *AAAI
Spring Symposium on Learning by Reading and Learning to Read*, Stanford, CA. 23

Palmer, Martha, Shijong Ryu, Jinyoung Choi, Sinwon Yoon, and Yeongmi Jeon. 2006. Korean
PropBank. OLAC Record oai:www.ldc.upenn.edu:LDC2006T03 53, 54

Philpot, Andrew, Eduard Hovy, and Patrick Pantel. 2005. The Omega Ontology. In the *Proceedings
of the IJCNLP Workshop on Ontologies and Lexical Resources (OntoLex-05)*, Jeju Island, South Korea.
23

Pradhan, Sameer, Kadri Hacioglu, Valerie Krugler, Wayne Ward, James H. Martin, and Daniel
Jurafsky. 2005. Support Vector Learning for Semantic Argument Classification. *Machine Learning*,
60(1):11–39. DOI: 10.1007/s10994-005-0912-2 32, 41, 42, 43, 45

Pradhan, Sameer, Honglin Sun, Wayne Ward, James H. Martin, and Daniel Jurafsky. 2004a. Parsing
Arguments of Nominalizations in English and Chinese. In *Proceedings of the Human Language
Technology Conference of the North American Chapter of the Association for Computational Linguistics:
(HLT/NAACL-04)*, pages 141–144, Boston, Mass. 75

Pradhan, Sameer, Wayne Ward, Kadri Hacioglu, James H. Martin, and Daniel Jurafsky. 2004b.
Shallow Semantic Parsing Using Support Vector Machines. In *Proceedings of the Human Language
Technology Conference of the North American Chapter of the Association for Computational Linguistics:
(HLT/NAACL-04)*, pages 233–240, Boston, Mass. 65

Pradhan, Sameer, Wayne Ward, Kadri Hacioglu, James H. Martin, and Daniel Jurafsky. 2005. Semantic Role Labeling Using Different Syntactic Views. In *Proceedings of the 43rd Annual Meeting of the Association for Computational Linguistics (ACL-05)*. DOI: 10.3115/1219840.1219912 47, 48, 49

Punyakanok, V., D. Roth, W. Yih, and D. Zimak. 2004. Semantic Role Labeling Via Integer Linear Programming Inference. In *Proceedings of the 20th International Conference on Computational Linguistics (COLING-04)*, pages 1346–1352, Geneva, Switzerland, August. DOI: 10.3115/1220355.1220552 45, 46

Rambow, Owen, Bonnie Dorr, Karin Kipper, Ivona Kucerova, and Martha Palmer. 2003. Automatically Deriving Tectogrammatical Labels From Other Resources: A Comparison of Semantic Labels From Other Resources. In *Prague Bulletin of Mathematical Linguistics*, volume 79-90, pages 23–35. 25

Ratnaparkhi, Adwait. 1997. A Linear Observed Time Statistical Parser Based on Maximum Entropy Models. In *Proceedings of the Second Conference on Empirical Methods in Natural Language Processing (EMNLP-97)*, pages 1–10, Providence, Rhode Island. ACL. 47

Roland, Douglas. 2001. *Verb Sense and Verb Subcategorization Probabilities*. Ph.D. thesis, University of Colorado, Boulder. 40

Rooth, Mats, Stefan Riezler, Detlef Prescher, Glenn Carroll, and Franz Beil. 1999. Inducing a Semantically Annotated Lexicon Via EM-Based Clustering. In *Proceedings of the 37th Annual Meeting of the Association for Computational Linguistics (ACL-99)*, pages 104–111, College Park, Maryland. DOI: 10.3115/1034678.1034703 42

Rosch, Eleanor H. 1973. Natural Categories. *Cognitive Psychology*, 4:328–350. DOI: 10.1016/0010-0285(73)90017-0 10

Saeed, John, (Ed.). 2003. *Semantics*. Blackwell Publishing, Malden, Mass. 3, 5

Schulte im Walde, Sabine. 2009. The Induction of Verb Frames and Verb Classes From Corpora. In Anke Ludeling and Merja Kyto, (Eds.), *Corpus Linguistics. An International Handbook*. Mouton de Gruyter, Berlin, pages 1–17. 18

Shen, Libin, Lucas Champollion, and Aravind Joshi. 2008. LTAG-Spinal and the TreeBank. *Language Resources and Evaluation*, 42:1–19. DOI: 10.1007/s10579-007-9043-7 47

Shen, Libin and Aravind Joshi. 2008. LTAG Dependency Parsing With Bidirectional Incremental Construction. In *Proceedings of the 2008 Conference on Empirical Methods in Natural Language Processing (EMNLP-08)*. 47

Shi, L. and R. Mihalcea. 2005. Putting Pieces Together: Combining FrameNet, VerbNet and WordNet for Robust Semantic Parsing. In *Proceedings of the 6th International Conference on Intelligent Text Processing and Computational Linguistics (CICLing)*, pages 100–111, Mexico City, Mexico. 50

Steedman, Mark. 2000. *The Syntactic Process*. The MIT Press, Cambridge Mass. 47

Subirats, Carlos and Miriam Petruck. 2003. Surprise! Spanish FrameNet! In *Proceedings of the Workshop on Frame Semantics at the XVII. International Congress of Linguists*, Prague, Czech. 54

Sun, Weiwei, Zhifang Sui, Meng Wang, and Xin Wang. 2009. Chinese Semantic role Labeling With Shallow Parsing. In *Proceedings of the 2009 Conference on Empirical Methods in Natural Language Processing (EMNLP-09)*, pages 1475–1483, Singapore, August. 68, 69

Surdeanu, Mihai, Sanda Harabagiu, John Williams, and Paul Aarseth. 2003. Using Predicate-Argument Structures for Information Extraction. In *Proceedings of the 41st Annual Meeting of the Association for Computational Linguistics (ACL-03)*, pages 8–15. DOI: 10.3115/1075096.1075098 41, 43

Surdeanu, Mihai, Richard Johansson, Adam Meyers, Lluís Màrquez, and Joakim Nivre. 2008. The CoNLL 2008 Shared Task on Joint Parsing of Syntactic and Semantic Dependencies. In *Proceedings of the Twelfth Conference on Computational Natural Language Learning (CoNLL-08)*, pages 159–177. 48, 50

Surdeanu, Mihai, Roser Morante, and Luis Màrquez. 2008. Analysis of Joint Inference Strategies for the Semantic Role labeling of Spanish and Catalan. In *Proceedings of the 9th International Conference on Intelligent Text Processing and Computational Linguistics (CICLing)*, Haifa, Israel. DOI: 10.1007/978-3-540-78135-6_18 53

Sutton, Charles and Andrew McCallum. 2005. Joint Parsing and Semantic Role Labeling. In *Proceedings of the Ninth Conference on Computational Natural Language Learning (CoNLL-05)*, pages 225–228. 47

Swier, Robert and Suzanne Stevenson. 2004. Unsupervised Semantic Role Labeling. In *Proceedings of 2004 Conference on Empirical Methods in Natural Language Processing (EMNLP-04)*. 52

Taulé, Mariona, M. A. Martí, , and Marta Recasens. 2008. AnCora: Mutlilevel Annotated Corpora for Catalan and Spanish. In *Proceedings of the Language Resources and Evaluation Conference (LREC-08)*, Marakech, Morocco. 53, 54

Toutanova, Kristina, Aria Haghighi, and Christopher Manning. 2005. Joint Learning Improves Semantic Role Labeling. In *Proceedings of the 43rd Annual Meeting of the Association for Computational Linguistics (ACL-05)*, pages 589–596. DOI: 10.3115/1219840.1219913 43, 44, 45

Wittgenstein, Ludwig. 1953/2001. *Philosophical Investigations*. Blackwell Publishing, Chichester, West Sussex, UK. 10

Xue, Nianwen. 2008. Labeling Chinese Predicates with Semantic Roles. *Computational Linguistics*, 34(2):225–255. DOI: 10.1162/coli.2008.34.2.225 53, 64, 65, 66, 67, 68, 72, 73

Xue, Nianwen and Martha Palmer. 2004. Calibrating features for Semantic Role Labeling. In *Proceedings of the 2004 Conference on Empirical Methods in Natural Language Processing (EMNLP-04)*, Barcelona, Spain. 33, 43, 65

Xue, Nianwen and Martha Palmer. 2005. Automatic Semantic Role Labeling for Chinese verbs. In *Proceedings of the Nineteenth International Joint Conference on Artificial Intelligence (IJCAI-05)*, pages 1160–1165, Edinburgh, Scotland. 74

Xue, Nianwen and Martha Palmer. 2009. Adding Semantic Roles to the Chinese TreeBank. *Natural Language Engineering*, 15(1):143–172. DOI: 10.1017/S1351324908004865 53, 54, 62

Xue, Nianwen, Fei Xia, Fu dong Chiou, and Martha Palmer. 2005. The Penn Chinese TreeBank: Phrase Structure Annotation of a Large Corpus. *Natural Language Engineering*, 11(2):207–238. DOI: 10.1017/S135132490400364X 65

Yi, Szu-Ting, Edward Loper, and Martha Palmer. 2007. Can Semantic Roles Generalize Across Genres? In *Proceedings of the Human Language Technology Conference/North American Chapter of the Association for Computational Linguistics Annual Meeting (HLT/NAACL-07)*. 51

Yi, Szu-ting and Martha Palmer. 2005. The Integration of Syntactic Parsing and Semantic Role Labeling. In *Proceedings of the Ninth Conference on Computational Natural Language Learning (CoNLL-05)*, pages 237–240. 47

Authors' Biographies

MARTHA PALMER

Martha Palmer is a Professor of Linguistics and Computer Science, and a Fellow of the Institute of Cognitive Science at the University of Colorado. Her current research is aimed at building domain-independent and language independent techniques for semantic interpretation based on linguistically annotated data used for training supervised systems, such as Proposition Banks. She has been the PI on projects to build Chinese, Korean and Hindi TreeBanks and English, Chinese, Korean, Arabic and Hindi Proposition Banks. She has been a member of the Advisory Committee for the DARPA TIDES program, Chair of SIGLEX, Chair of SIGHAN, and is a past President of the Association for Computational Linguistics. She was formerly an Associate Professor in Computer and Information Sciences at the University of Pennsylvania and received her Ph.D. in Artificial Intelligence from the University of Edinburgh in 1985.

DANIEL GILDEA

Daniel Gildea is an Associate Professor of Computer Science at the University of Rochester. His research focuses on statistical approaches to natural language processing, in particular for the tasks of machine translation and language understanding. He received his Ph.D. in computer science from UC Berkeley in 2001 and was a postdoctoral scholar at the University of Pennsylvania for two years before coming to Rochester.

NIANWEN XUE

Nianwen Xue is an Assistant Professor of Languages & Linguistics and Computer Science at Brandeis University. His research interests include syntactic and semantic parsing, temporal representation and inference, Chinese language processing, and linguistic annotation (Chinese Treebank, Chinese Proposition Bank, OntoNotes). He received his PhD in linguistics from University of Delaware in 2001, and was a postdoctoral researcher at the Department of Computer and Information Science of University of Pennsylvania. He held an Assistant Research Professor position at the University of Colorado at Boulder before joining Brandeis.

Printed in the United States
by Baker & Taylor Publisher Services